SEE YOU
at the
CAMPGROUND

SEE YOU
at the
CAMPGROUND

A Guide to Discovering Community,
Connection, and a Happier Family
in the Great Outdoors

Stephanie & Jeremy Puglisi

Chapter 12: Campground Etiquette was originally published in a slightly different form in the November 2017 issue of *Trailer Life Magazine*.

This publication is designed to provide accurate and authoritative information in regard to the subject matter covered. It is sold with the understanding that the publisher is not engaged in rendering legal, accounting, or other professional service. If legal advice or other expert assistance is required, the services of a competent professional person should be sought.—*From a Declaration of Principles Jointly Adopted by a Committee of the American Bar Association and a Committee of Publishers and Associations*

All brand names and product names used in this book are trademarks, registered trademarks, or trade names of their respective holders. Sourcebooks is not associated with any product or vendor in this book.

Published by Sourcebooks
P.O. Box 4410, Naperville, Illinois 60567-4410
(630) 961-3900
sourcebooks.com

Library of Congress Cataloging-in-Publication data is on file with the publisher.

Printed and bound in the United States of America.
SB 10 9 8 7 6 5 4 3 2 1

To Theo, Max, and Wes

You have inspired us to create a life
bigger than we ever imagined. Thank
you for exploring the world with us.

CONTENTS

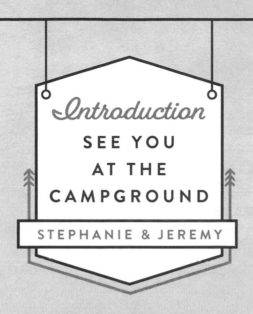

Introduction

SEE YOU AT THE CAMPGROUND

STEPHANIE & JEREMY

This is supposed to be a book about camping. And it is. Mostly.

We promise to share the highs and lows of our family camping experiences over the past ten years. We'll give you the best tips and tricks we know for finding the perfect campgrounds and planning amazing camping vacations. The words "camping" and "campground" will be used *a lot*. We pinky swear. Hand to heart. Scout's honor.

But in reality, this story isn't about the types of recreational vehicles (RVs), tents, or cabins we have stayed in over the last decade. It's about the journey. The view out the window. The couple trying to figure out their marriage. The little kids buckled up in the back seat. The rescue pup on the floor of the truck waiting patiently for yummy crumbs to fall. It's about all the lessons we have learned and are still learning.

It's about two parents who were trying to figure out what a happy family life actually looked like, since they didn't have much of a track record to draw on. It's about two high school sweethearts who knew they loved each other and didn't know a whole heck of a lot else about life. In a random twist of fate, desperately grasping at straws, they said, "Hey, let's buy a pop-up camper."

In hindsight, it's hard to say why we landed on this particular solution to our particular problem. Our relationship was on the rocks, and being the parents of twin babies was giving us a run for our money. We knew that we needed to bring some serious fun back into our lives. But a pop-up camper? Really? Most reasonable people would just start going to the gym or put some date nights on the calendar.

Well, we decided to pick up camping as our new family hobby and ended up transforming ourselves, our marriage, and our family life. Sometimes we feel pretty silly talking about how a little pop-up camper changed our lives. But we say it anyway, because it's true.

Maybe you find yourself in the same situation we were in. We mostly loved our home. We mostly loved our jobs. We were attached to many of our little daily routines, like enjoying coffee and breakfast sandwiches at the playground on Saturday mornings.

But we also wanted more. As soon as we became parents, we felt this immediate pressure to dive into a lifestyle full of "family-friendly activities." It seemed like all the normal parents filled their weekends with Touch-A-Truck events, Chuck E. Cheese's birthday parties, and endless, but necessary, household chores. As we slipped into these routines and patterns in our family life, we were left feeling bored, restless, and stressed out.

So we decided to stop trying to fit into someone else's mold. We decided the great outdoors was big and full of opportunities for adventure. We decided outside was probably a better place for our loud and energetic kids than inside some plastic play center. We decided we could have just as much fun with kids as we'd had as a couple before they were born. We just had to write our own script. And our script included a pop-up camper.

In the last decade, we've spent hundreds of nights camping with our kids. We've taken them to national parks, urban destinations, historical monuments, and sandy beaches. We've camped in rustic state parks and off-the-hook luxury campground resorts. All three of our boys learned to ride their bikes at campgrounds. They also learned to fish, hike, kayak, and paddleboard. We've tent camped on the Oregon coast and towed an RV to Mount Rushmore. We've eaten tacos in Texas and lobsters in Maine. Sometimes we joke that our boys experienced more in the first ten years of their lives than either of us did in our first three decades.

For our family, the campground has become a place where we disconnect from the demands of daily life and reconnect with each other. It's a place where we enjoy time with friends or just spend a quiet weekend together. It can be a base camp for exploring new destinations or a familiar place we return to year after year. The campground is where we start the day eating breakfast at the picnic table and end the day making s'mores around the campfire. The campground is a place for us to be together without the countless distractions of to-do lists, projects, and devices.

The script you choose to write for your family might be a bit different, and that's okay. You don't need an RV to step off the hamster wheel of daily life and find fun and adventure with your family in the great outdoors. You don't need to take an epic cross-country road trip or even leave your home state. You might just decide to dust off that old tent or try out a cabin rental at a nearby campground.

If you are looking to call a time-out for your family and take a break from the endless tasks and responsibilities of day-to-day life, we'll help you forge a new path. We want to inspire you to get outside, play in the dirt, and have fun together. See new sights. Learn new things. Take that road trip you've been dreaming about. It can feel a bit overwhelming, but our practical tips and real-life experiences will help you do it all without losing your mind.

We know life is busy. We know there are bathrooms to clean, lawns to mow, and endless piles of laundry to wash. But there are also mountains to climb, fish to catch, and campfires to build. So in the midst of all the busyness, we hope you are inspired to escape to the campground every once in a while.

The campground is a special place for our family. Time slows down, the noisiness of life fades into the background, and we connect as a family in the simplest ways possible, through cooking a meal over a campfire or playing a card game at the picnic table.

We are also intimately familiar with all the roadblocks that keep families from getting to this place. We know that it can seem overwhelming to plan camping trips, research an RV purchase, pack for a family vacation, and survive that road trip with your kids. This book will make tackling all of those details as simple as possible. We've done it the hard way at times and learned a lot of valuable lessons that we're happy to pass along.

So here's the road map that we've used to find adventure and joy on our journey as a family. We hope it helps make your own journey a bit easier...and a lot more fun.

We'll see you at the campground.

CHAPTER

One

REASONS
Camping Vacations
ARE BETTER

STEPHANIE

The first few decades of our lives were rather unremarkable. Jeremy and I were classic high school sweethearts who got married right after college and immediately dove into our professional careers as educators. We hopped around the country a bit as we earned our master's degrees but ultimately ended up settling in the same place where we were both born and raised—the Jersey Shore.

As we inched toward our thirties, we checked off all the typical boxes. We suffered through terrible first jobs that barely paid for ramen noodle dinners. We lived in a professor's cramped attic apartment and a grandparent's basement as we struggled to pay off student loans. We eventually found better paying jobs and finally bought a house.

Our lives were fairly typical for a young married couple living in the suburbs of New Jersey. Except for one thing: we were total road warriors. We simply loved road trips. We'd fill up the car with gas, pop in our favorite mixtape, and drive for hours and hours.

Our first official road trip took place back when we were still teenagers and decided on a whim to head south to the New Orleans Jazz & Heritage Festival. We stayed in the diviest hostel imaginable, got pulled over by the

Alabama police on the way home, and got our car broken into the night before we finally made it home. It was the best trip ever.

Over the next few years, most of our road trips involved driving back and forth to each other's colleges. I went to school in Michigan and Jeremy stayed in New Jersey, so we both became pros at clocking eleven hours behind the wheel without breaking a sweat.

In later years, we drove cross-country so Jeremy could attend graduate school in California. And when my immediate family relocated to North Carolina, we would drive to the beautiful Blue Ridge Mountains from New Jersey at least three times a year.

Sometimes I wonder if it all really started there. So many of the most exciting moments of our lives happened when we got behind the wheel and drove. I think that, over the years, road trips became deeply connected with our idea of adventure as a couple.

Then everything got a bit more complicated. Our twin boys, Max and Theo, were born in May 2009. We were both teachers at the time, so the whole summer stretched in front of us, and we had absolutely no idea how to fill it up.

Before kids came along, our summers had been jam-packed with side gigs, a little bit of travel, and a lot of beach time. Now, with two newborn babies, we certainly weren't going to work a summer job or plan a road trip. But sitting on the beach relaxing with the boys seemed like a reasonable prospect. Until we tried it a few times.

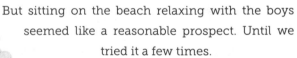

Now let's be clear. Plenty of people take their newborns to the beach and have a lovely time. We just aren't those people. It was so much work for so very little reward. We would spend hours packing everything up and figuring out how to get it all down to the beach without dropping a baby in the process. Then we would huddle under the umbrella, rocking or feeding the boys and trying not to get sand in their eyes. The saddest part of all was when we had to take turns going for a swim in the ocean, one at a time, while the other sat on the blanket hoping that both babies didn't start crying at the same time.

There were definitely sweet moments when we walked down the shoreline with both boys napping in carriers, but those were the exception, not the rule. Two weeks into summer, we admitted to each other that we weren't particularly enjoying our time off as a brand-new family. It was time to shift gears.

Our summers before kids had always included some sort of road-trip adventure. We rarely flew anywhere, preferring to load up the car and drive twelve hours at a clip, often through the night. We loved playing music, listening to our favorite radio programs, and stopping at divey roadside joints for pancakes at midnight. That summer, sometime in early July, we sat on the floor of our living room, each of us holding a two-month-old baby, trying to figure out what we were going to do with the next seven weeks. Then one of us suggested a road trip.

We don't remember who said it first, but either way, we were both on board immediately. Sure, it seemed a little crazy. The same people who were getting stressed out going to the beach with newborn twins were now going to go on vacation. Yet, in another way, it made perfect sense. The learning curve for becoming a parent is pretty steep, but there was one lesson we had learned quickly: relaxing and having fun look very different once you have kids. You can't just expect to go to the beach, surf a few waves, and read a good book while soaking up some rays.

But something inside of us was certain that we could still have fun. We just had to recalibrate and shift our notion of what it meant to relax and enjoy time together. We were also picking up on a simple truth about our boys that remains true to this day. Even as tiny babies, they were at their best when we were moving and having an adventure. Sitting still doesn't suit them now, and it didn't suit them when they were two months old. Whenever they would get fussy, a walk or a car ride would calm them right down.

So it really didn't seem crazy to think about a road trip with newborns. Sitting around attempting to enjoy the lazy days of summer just wasn't working. It was time to try another approach.

¤

Since my parents had relocated to North Carolina, the Asheville area had become one of our favorite road-trip destinations. So that afternoon, sitting on the floor of the living room with napping babies on our chests, we decided to make the thirteen-hour drive down to the Blue Ridge Mountains.

What could go wrong? We had done that drive dozens of times in the past, and my parents had a spare bedroom where we could all camp out for a couple of weeks. Asheville is full of amazing live music, awesome restaurants, and beautiful hikes just a short drive from downtown. It was like "Fun Times" was flashing in neon lights right before our very eyes. It is no exaggeration to say that twenty-four hours later, the car was packed, and we were headed south.

Now, Max and Theo were just about two months old at this point. We didn't exactly have the whole *baby* thing dialed in yet, much less the whole *drive-for-thirteen-hours-with-two-babies-on-board* thing. Looking back, it's hard to believe that we made it down to North Carolina in one piece.

Because the boys had napped so well in the car around town, we'd probably figured that they would just sleep away the thirteen-hour drive. Of course, that's not what happened. The boys took turns crying *for the entire drive*. And it hadn't occurred to us that the journey would take two hours longer, since we had to stop to feed the newborns constantly. But we survived. Barely. And I may or may not have bought noise-canceling headphones for the ride home a couple of weeks later.

This was the very first time we tried to have an adventure with our kids, and we learned a lot, because to be completely honest, it was a bit of a disaster. First of all, staying in a spare room in your parents' house with newborn twins is not as easy as it may seem. Our boys were terrible sleepers, and we felt awful that they were waking up the whole household multiple times every night. My parents probably didn't mean to make us feel guilty, but the bleary-eyed breakfasts where everyone recounted how many times they were woken up the night before left us feeling like interlopers in someone else's territory.

Then there was the shocking realization that it's a little more difficult to enjoy upscale restaurants and urban nightlife with a couple of newborns in tow. Jeremy would pore over the weekly *Mountain Xpress* and silently come to terms with all the bands that he would not be seeing during our stay.

Yes, we probably should have had more realistic expectations about our activity schedule. And there might have been a tiny piece of me that was expecting my family to share some of the baby-caretaking burden, which didn't end up happening. Nobody insisted on babysitting while we went out for the first time since having the boys. That's okay, since nobody owes you free babysitting in life. Unfortunately, it's a lesson many of us have to learn the hard way.

All told, a lot of parents might have walked away from the experience feeling defeated by their first attempt at an epic family adventure. Not us. We are professionally trained teachers who seem to be compelled to view everything in life as a learning experience. For most of the ride home—whenever I wasn't wearing my noise-canceling headphones—we dissected the ins and outs of the Great Family Road Trip of 2009. A couple of big takeaways kept coming up over and over.

First, we had a ton of fun doing things that we hadn't done a lot in the past. Hiking, for one. Some of our greatest memories from that trip are of strapping the boys into their BabyBjörn carriers and finding great walking trails around Mount Mitchell. FYI, the Balsam Nature Trail at the summit of Mount Mitchell loops through a fairy-tale fir forest, and the hike is the perfect length for a newborn's nap.

And second: road food. We gained a new appreciation on this trip for roadside barbecue joints with outdoor picnic tables and plenty of room for our BOB two-seat jogging stroller. Noise and mess are par for the course in this environment, which suited us perfectly. Our obsession with finding great places to eat has only grown throughout the years. It's amazing to look back and realize that our family tradition of seeking out the best road-food joints around the country started a decade ago at 12 Bones Smokehouse in Arden, North Carolina.

So as we pulled into our driveway in New Jersey, we were exhausted (of course!) but also delighted with ourselves for coming up with our next big idea. Traveling with the twins was obviously an awesome experience, worth the hard work and effort. We just needed to pivot away from the whole extended-family thing and have our own space, perhaps in a...hotel, right? Like most ideas conceived after a fifteen-hour car ride, this ended up being a bad one. But we were totally committed. Life was busy as the next school year kicked off and we both went back to work. There wasn't time for any more *amazing family adventures*, but soon enough that claustrophobic feeling started to kick in, and we were looking at each other and asking, "What should we *do*? Where should we *go*?"

At this point, we thought we knew everything. First of all, getting out of the house and shaking up the routine with our boys was a good thing. Second, staying in someone else's house with infant twins was a bad thing. So we decided to take advantage of a well-timed Groupon deal. We nabbed a room at the CoCo Key Water Resort, a hotel that was only two hours away and...wait for it...had an on-site water park! The plan was to pair some kid-friendly fun with nearby urban shopping and dining.

Enter the hotel stay from hell. It's hard to imagine if you haven't experienced it personally. The sheer horror of watching crawling babies put their hands and mouths on every single filthy thing still sends shivers down our spines. Every item in the hotel room was a potential danger, so we spent the entirety of our time in the room chasing the boys around and making sure they didn't eat the carpet fuzz.

And then there was bedtime. Max and Theo were always early risers, which also meant that they were a special kind of torture past 7:00 p.m. So there we were, at normal people's dinnertime, drawing the curtains, turning on the noise machine, and shushing our living brains out to get the tiny terrors to sleep. They would start drifting off and then someone would run down the hall yelling. Their eyes would fly open, and unseemly words would fly out of our mouths. Televisions, elevators, room service—you don't realize how much noise there is in a hotel until you try to put a baby to sleep in one. After what seemed like hours, the boys were finally asleep, and we were giving each other quiet fist bumps in the pitch-black hotel room.

It took a minute for reality to set in. Max and Theo were out like lights, and we wanted them to stay that way. So the next few hours of our lives would entail remaining absolutely silent in a dark hotel room. There's an exciting Saturday night for you.

Twenty minutes later, we were perched on the edge of the bathroom tub, drinking ginger ale, eating pretzels, and sharing a single set of earphones as we watched back-to-back episodes of *Top Chef* on our laptop. The epic sadness of the moment was not lost on us. In fact, years later we can still feel the disappointment of that hotel stay deep in our bones. If we had a picture of us in that moment, it would be best captioned, "Oh, how the mighty have fallen."

In the morning, we packed up our bags and a ridiculous amount of baby gear and drove home before most of the other hotel guests were even awake.

¤

That hotel-from-hell adventure took place in late fall. That was the last time we set foot in a hotel with our boys for many, many years, until we could be sure that no one would eat the carpet fuzz. But on the drive home that day, we started hammering out plans for our next big idea: the family pop-up camper.

Jeremy and I might have been road warriors, but we were definitely not seasoned campers. We had both had just enough camping experiences throughout the years to imagine that a pop-up camper would be the answer to the question of how we were going to have epic adventures with our little kids in tow.

When I was growing up, my father was a contractor who worked hard and rarely took time off. He was also an Eagle Scout, so when we did take the rare family vacation, it involved a mint-green station wagon, a giant army-issued canvas tent, and a platoon of red Coleman coolers stuffed with food my mother would prepare for weeks in advance. Most years, we would head to Assateague State Park in Maryland for an end-of-summer camping trip with family friends. Sometimes my parents borrowed a pop-up camper from some folks we knew pretty well.

As a result of my childhood, a pop-up camper seemed like the pinnacle of luxury. You see, us kids weren't even allowed inside. We had to stay in that eight-man army tent while my parents enjoyed the comfort of dry, elevated mattresses. I remember standing in the doorway, peeking in, imagining how good life would be if we could just sleep in that pop-up camper instead of in a damp, musty sleeping bag.

I think that idea stuck with me for decades afterward. In my mind, a pop-up camper was a comfortable little hotel on wheels that you could take to beautiful places like Assateague State Park. I had floated this idea to Jeremy over the years, but it had never really gained any traction. It took a couple of really bad travel experiences with infants for my pop-up camper idea to actually stick.

See, we weren't just struggling to be parents. We were also struggling to be a couple. In some ways, Jeremy and I had always been that "opposites attract" kind of couple, and that worked okay when it was just the two of us. I was a morning person; he was a night owl. He liked to go out; I loved to stay in. I went to yoga on Saturdays while Jeremy went to play basketball. We ping-ponged off of each other, enjoying time together and then going off and enjoying our own version of fun. Having twins challenged that dynamic. Anytime that one of us was solo with two babies, it felt like the loneliest and longest time in the world. We experienced all the typical stress points for young parents: juggling work and childcare, middle-of-the-night wakings, and the never-ending parade of sicknesses.

Over the previous decade, my entire immediate and extended family had moved out of the state of New Jersey. To be honest, their absence hadn't affected us too strongly before we had kids. We visited a few times a year and talked on the phone daily. Jeremy and I were busy in our careers and lives. But when the twins arrived, loneliness and isolation became an acute condition for both Jeremy and me. We knew we loved each other, but it was hard to really connect as a couple while feeling so overwhelmed by our daily circumstances.

Our tenth wedding anniversary was looming on the horizon, and it felt very symbolic to both of us. Would our marriage survive this shift from being a couple to being parents? We both needed some grand, romantic gesture, and a luxurious European getaway was simply not in the cards. But a pop-up camper? We could definitely swing that.

Over the course of the winter, Jeremy dove into the research, since he is the shopper in our relationship. I mostly stayed out of the process, because spending money stresses me out. We never even considered other RV options. A pop-up camper was affordable, it could fit in our very small driveway, and it could be towed by our Toyota Highlander SUV. Done, done, and done.

By April, just a month before the boys celebrated their first birthday, Jeremy was backing a brand-new pop-up camper into the driveway. We weren't giving up. That pop-up camper wasn't just an RV. It was our all-in bet. We were putting all the chips on the table and crossing our fingers for a big win. We were a family, and darn it, we wanted to be a happy one.

Reasons Camping Vacations Are Better

These days, we give a lot of educational seminars at RV shows, and over the last few years, we've met hundreds of families who are wondering if camping is right for them. Some of them camped when they were growing up and are looking to share that experience with their own kids. Other folks have never pitched a tent in their lives but are looking to take a deep breath, call a time-out on the hectic pace of daily life, and spend more quality time with the family. Like us, they've had their fair share of experiences with hotels and Airbnbs, and they're curious about a different type of family vacation.

We've certainly tried it all over the years, and here are the reasons we love camping vacations more than any other type of travel. If these reasons resonate with you, then you're on the right path.

Camping Lets You Spend Less and Travel More

When we bought our first RV, we were two teachers with plenty of time to travel but not a lot of disposable income. Camping allows us to control our expenses more than any other form of travel. We can drive shorter distances to save money on gas, prepare our own meals to save money on food, and stay in state and national parks to save money on campsites.

The RV industry claims that RV vacations are about 50 percent cheaper than traditional vacations that include airline tickets and hotel accommodations. As we've tracked our expenses over the years, we've found that this is absolutely accurate for our travel budget. Even if we splurge on some resort camping experiences and a couple of meals out, our camping vacations remain about half the total cost of other family travel that we do throughout the year.

--------- **Cost Comparisons for Camping Vacations** ---------

According to a 2018 study conducted by CBRE Hotels Advisory Group, RV vacations cost much less than other types of vacation travel, even when factoring in fuel prices and the cost of RV ownership. The study found cost savings of 21–64 percent for a four-person family, while a two-person family saves 8–53 percent, depending on factors such as the type of RV, distance traveled, and accommodations.

Average Cost for a Seven-Day Trip

RVing: $1,993	RVing: $1,993	RVing: $1,993
vs.	vs.	vs.
Drive/hotel rental: $2,956	Fly/drive/hotel rental: $4,113	Fly/drive/house rental: $3,114

Campers Are Social People

It's no secret that a lot of families are struggling to find community these days. Many of us move to new locations for work or have family spread out around the country. It's hard to make new friends while you're busy working and raising kids.

When we started camping, we didn't know anyone else who camped on a regular basis. However, that changed quickly enough. Campgrounds are a bit like neighborhoods of the past. Everyone is outside, waving as you walk by, and perfectly willing to stop and chat about the weather. We have met families at the campground who have become actual, real-life friends.

We recently spent the weekend at a nearby campground with eight other families, none of whom we knew before we bought the pop-up camper. All the kids spent their time riding bikes, fishing, and playing whiffle ball. The adults sat around the campfire talking and laughing for hours. Where else does that happen these days?

Campgrounds Offer Tons of Room to Roam

Campgrounds allow us to enjoy our time with the kids because we are not constantly trying to control their activity levels. Our boys love to run and jump and move, and campgrounds offer plenty of space for those sorts of shenanigans. In hotels or rented houses, we're always trying to stop our kids from running inside, jumping on the beds, and wrestling on the couch. At the campground, they can ride their bikes, run around at the playground, or play catch in the field. The outdoor space is a game changer for our family.

Yes, we love the cost savings of camping. But given the choice between an equally priced hotel room or campground, we would still choose camping every time because of the value of that outdoor space for our family.

Many Campgrounds Offer On-Site Activities and Entertainment

The first time I priced out an all-inclusive getaway vacation for the family, my jaw dropped. I realized that a week on a Caribbean island would just about suck up all of our travel funds for the entire year. We never ended up taking that type of vacation because we discovered the world of resort campgrounds and never looked back.

You might get sticker shock when you find out that there are campsites that cost $100 a night, but that price might actually be a steal when you consider the on-site activities and amenities included. Our favorite resort campgrounds have multiple pools, hot tubs, waterslides, lazy rivers, and mini golf. Many have daily schedules jam-packed with ice-cream socials, T-shirt tie-dyeing, and whiffle-ball tournaments. At these campgrounds, we can arrive, set up camp, and stay at the resort for the entire vacation. It's our own affordable version of that all-inclusive Caribbean getaway that we never experienced.

> Families are spending more time camping than ever before, citing the motivation to be outdoors.
>
> (Kampgrounds of America (KOA), 2018 North American Camping Report)

Nightly Campfire Time Is Heaven

If you are anything like us, date nights are few and far between. At home, we put the kids to bed and then flop down, exhausted, in front of our separate screens. Even if we are in the same room, we're lost in our respective social media feeds or latest Netflix binges. The same thing occurs when we stay in hotel rooms with the kids. Lights go out, headphones go on, and we might as well be miles away from each other.

The very first time we went camping, something magical happened. The babies fell asleep, and we found ourselves sitting around the campfire, simply chatting. It was the closest we had come to a real date in a very long time. Years later, our kids don't go to bed so early anymore. But that's okay. We cherish campfire time just as much now that we all enjoy it together.

No matter how hard we try, we never manage to replicate that campfire magic when we're at home, distracted by our endless to-do lists and easy access to technology. The campfire has become a sacred place in our family...the place where we talk, laugh, sing songs, and eat s'mores.

It's Easy to Travel with Family and Friends

Many campgrounds offer cabins, tenting areas, and RV sites, so there are different accommodations for anyone who wants to come along. We've had grandparents and neighbors stay in cabins while we parked our RV next door. We've done big, fun adventures where ten kids had a sleepover in one tent. Oftentimes, we'll let our friends know that we've booked a spot at a local campground for an upcoming weekend. By the time the weekend rolls around, we'll have three or four other families joining us.

We can all enjoy each other's company, sharing meals and competing in rowdy cornhole tournaments. Then we retreat to the comfort of our own space at the end of the day. It's been a wonderful way for us to build relationships with our friends and family over the years.

Top Reasons People Say They Go Camping

1. Camping is a time to just relax and not feel like I have to be somewhere or do something.

2. Camping is a great way for me to escape the stress of everyday life.

3. Camping allows me to clear my mind.

4. I like to camp as part of a group of friends and family.

5. Camping is an affordable vacation option.

(KOA, 2018 North American Camping Report)

You Can Bring Your Four-Legged Friends

Camping is ridiculously pet friendly. It's estimated that more than 50 percent of people who own an RV also travel with at least one pet. I always knew that we would eventually want to bring a dog into the family, since I had grown up with a gaggle of dogs and cats. When the time was right to adopt, it was such a relief that we could bring Maggie along on our camping adventures instead of putting her in doggie day care every time we wanted to travel. It turns out that Maggie might just be the biggest camping fanatic in the family. She lives for long walks around the campground and is by far the most enthusiastic hiker out of all of us.

You Can Bring Your Own Food

We love a lot of things about camping trips, but this might be the one that is most important to us day in and day out. Eating all your meals out while traveling is expensive and exhausting with kids. It can also be unhealthy. But we can pack all our favorite foods in our RV's kitchen or in coolers before we leave on a trip. Plus, we can even prepare lunch at a rest stop on a travel day without ever having to go into those yucky fast-food joints.

This is one of the primary reasons that we will choose a cabin over a hotel room when we aren't traveling with our RV. Now that we know what it's like to have a kitchen while traveling, it's very hard for us to go without one. We've become completely spoiled—we love having home-cooked meals no matter where we are.

You Get to Reconnect with Nature

I don't need an expert to tell me that we all spend too much time indoors and on our devices. The studies just tell us what we already know. We should be taking more walks and spending more time looking at the stars, but life somehow gets in the way. It's amazing how much more time you naturally spend outdoors when you are camping, even if you're staying in a cabin or RV. We eat breakfast at the picnic table, the kids run around at the playground, and we relax around the campfire at night. At home, our bikes stay in the garage for days at a time. At the campground, we ride them many times a day. Our dog gets walked more, and we take the time to relax in the hammock.

To be completely frank, I think our boys spend more time outside when we are at home *because* of all the time spent outside at the campground. Over the years, they've learned to create their own fun out in nature, and I believe that has helped us in the constant battle against screen time. Sure, I have to turn off the TV and kick my kids outside just like any other parent. But they sure do know what to do with themselves once they're out there.

We first bought our pop-up camper because we wanted to road-trip in comfort, traveling with our own bed, gear, and food. It didn't take long for us to discover that there were so many more benefits to camping than we had realized. Now, whether we are traveling with our RV or flying to a destination, we know that campgrounds are the right choice for our family.

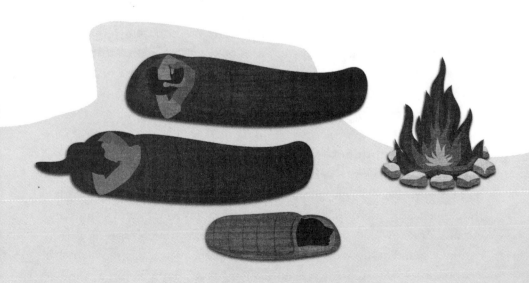

Health Benefits of Camping

Various studies have proven the many health benefits of camping, including:

- more fresh air
- less stress
- better sleep
- more vitamin D
- higher activity levels

CHAPTER

Two

Choose Your Own

CAMPING
ADVENTURE

JEREMY

When Stephanie and I first bought that pop-up camper, we had no idea that American camping was entering a new golden age. In many ways, there has never been a better time to go camping. According to the *2019 North American Camping Report* by Kampgrounds of America (KOA), there are nearly seventy-nine million camping "households" in the United States. Some of these families are tent campers, some are cabin campers, and others are RV owners. But no matter how they go camping, they have a wider variety of options for accommodations, experiences, and gear than any generation has had before. Right now is the perfect time for you to pitch a tent, hitch up an RV, or rent a cabin and take your seat around the campfire.

There is no wrong way to go camping. The only mistake you can make is staying home.

Tent campers no longer have to deal with the leaky and antiquated canvas tents of the 1970s and '80s. In fact, they don't even need to sleep on the ground anymore. Cots and sleeping pads that are specifically designed for tenting have dramatically increased the comfort of a night spent in the woods. Today's tents are also surprisingly lightweight and waterproof. You don't have to worry about touching the canvas sides and flooding the tent like you did back in the '80s.

RV ownership among Americans is also at an all-time high. This is largely because purchasing an RV is more affordable than it has ever been. After the Great Recession, many manufacturers began making a wider variety of lighter, less expensive RVs that can be towed by small pickup trucks, SUVs, and even the family minivan. Just walk around your neighborhood and take a look; there are probably RV owners living right on your block.

Many Americans still associate the word "RV" with expensive motorhomes purchased by older folks after retirement (or with Cousin Eddie from *National Lampoon's Christmas Vacation*). But these are outdated notions. The average age of RV owners has declined significantly over the last decade. The van-life movement has also exploded in recent years among millennials who are eager to hit the open road and embrace experience over consumerism. Many of these millennials witnessed their parents get burned in the housing crisis over a decade ago, and they have decided to avoid buying homes (at least for the time being) and to redefine the American dream by living a nomadic life on the road. Their camper vans run the gamut from remodeled Volkswagen Westfalias that were salvaged from the scrap heap to brand-new Winnebagos with price tags that can easily reach $100K. If you are looking for travel inspiration, just search for #vanlife on Instagram—the dusty back roads and byways of the American West will burst to life and jump right off your screen. While these van lifers often skip traditional campgrounds for more remote, off-grid, "boondocking" spots, the RV industry is betting big that, once they get a little bit older and have children of their own, we will see them at the campground en masse in shiny new travel trailers and motorhomes.

As interest in the great outdoors continues to grow, so do cabin-camping options. Those who want basic accommodations with a bed and roof over their heads can rent an affordable rustic cabin and find their inner Thoreau. Families who want a more luxurious experience can rent deluxe or premium cabins with kitchens, bathrooms, temperature control capabilities, and even flat-screen TVs. Your crusty old Uncle Joe might tell you that you're not really "camping" at this point, but have you ever listened to his advice anyway?

Options for stylish and uniquely outfitted rentals, such as glamping tents, yurts, and teepees, have also exploded over the past decade. When the term "glamping" (short for "glamorous camping") first appeared around 2005, it was often ridiculed by old guard tent campers and RV owners like Uncle Joe. But what initially started as a trend is starting to harden into an industry with real staying power. The recently launched American Glamping Association seeks to band together the growing number of campground owners who are offering (and profiting nicely from) these diverse and lavish accommodations. We have glamped in luxurious, fully furnished canvas tents along the coasts of Oregon and Maine and loved every second of it. If camping in a tent or towing your own RV is not right for you at the moment, a glamping experience might just fit the bill. But be prepared—the bill might be larger than you think! Hundreds of campgrounds are adding these types of deluxe accommodations, often right next door to their humbler tent and RV sites. The current diversity of campground accommodations is truly remarkable—there is something for everyone at every price point. And when I say "everyone," I actually mean everyone. This is where the new golden age of American camping departs from its last iteration—and thankfully so.

The first great golden age of American camping happened right after World War II and extended into the 1960s.

More than half of campers say they'd like to go glamping in the coming year.

(KOA, 2019 North American Camping Report)

Thousands of veterans returning from the war decided to "See America First" with their young families—and many of them chose to do so in tents and RVs, or while camping out of their cars and shiny new station wagons. Many state and national park campgrounds were brand-new at that point—as was much of the interstate highway system (a.k.a. the Dwight D. Eisenhower National System of Interstate and Defense Highways). Private campgrounds began to thrive in this era too, as enterprising individuals saw an opportunity to capitalize on the increase in highway travel. The Kampgrounds of America franchise system, for example, which is now the largest in the country, was first established in Billings, Montana, after businessman Dave Drum observed waves of travelers passing through town on their way to the 1962 World's Fair in Seattle. It truly was a golden age for road-tripping and American camping.

We have to point out that, at that time, the vast majority of those campers were white. Today, campgrounds are becoming increasingly diverse. When we first started camping a decade ago, it was unusual to see minority families at the campground. In many parts of America, that trend is quickly becoming part of the past. According to racial and ethnic demographics reported in KOA's *2019 North American Camping Report*, new campers who are just entering the lifestyle are actually more diverse than the overall U.S. population. Campgrounds are starting to look a lot more like America, and we couldn't be happier about that fact.

No matter who you are, or where you come from, we hope to see you at the campground. Heaven knows we spend a lot of time there ourselves. Our family usually heads to the campground in our own RV, but we have also rented cabins and stayed in tents. We love all of these options for a variety of reasons, and we think you should consider each of them seriously for your next family vacation. The diversity of accommodations at today's campgrounds are more robust than ever—but most Americans still take their first camping trip in a tent. And that's where it all started for me more than three decades ago.

Tent-Camping Adventures

Tent camping is thought of as a classic American pastime. Many parents purchase tents because of their own personal and sentimental childhood memories of pitching them in the woods with Mom and Dad. That's definitely not the case for me. I never went camping with either of my parents.

My father was a drinker, and we didn't have money for family trips. In fact, my one memory of camping as a kid was with my friend and his father. When I was in third grade, they invited me on a weekend trip with their Cub Scout den. I said yes without hesitation. But in the weeks leading up to the trip, I bounced back and forth between excitement and anxiety.

The thought of playing manhunt and roasting marshmallows under the stars was exciting. But I had no idea how to pitch a tent, set up camp, or build a fire. So my inexperience made me anxious.

I clearly remember the hustle and bustle of arriving at the campground on a crisp fall night. Tents were being pitched. A campfire was being built. Lanterns were glowing in warm circles on picnic tables. But most importantly, hamburgers and hot dogs were being cooked over camp stoves. They were green, two-burner Coleman camp stoves, and every single one of the men seemed to own one. Now I own a few of them myself. But back then, this ritual and the gear involved were entirely foreign and exotic to me. I was in complete awe.

My only other memory from that first night of camping was waking up in the middle of the night and having to pee. The thought of stepping over piles of unfamiliar bodies and figuring out how to unzip the tent left me totally paralyzed. I held it in and tried, without much luck, to fall back asleep. It was a long night, to stay the least. I woke up feeling thankful that I hadn't peed my pants. Small victories, right?

> ------------ **Tips for Your First Tent-Camping Trip** ------------
>
> ✧ Don't spend a ton of money on gear until you know you love tent camping.
>
> ✧ Consider borrowing or renting tents and gear for your first trip.
>
> ✧ Camp close to home.
>
> ✧ Pick a state or county park if you want natural beauty.
>
> ✧ Read online reviews of whatever campground you choose to make sure it's a good fit.
>
> ✧ Bring a quality first aid kit and scout out the location of the nearest hospital and emergency services.
>
> ✧ Pick a temperate time of year. Your first trip will be more enjoyable if your kids aren't shivering or sweating all night long.
>
> ✧ Learn how to properly pack a cooler and dry food.

My first tent-camping weekend was far from a smashing success. But it lit a fire somewhere deep in my belly. I swore to myself that I would go camping again. Unfortunately, it would be eight years before I went on another camping trip. I bought a tent during my senior year of high school and promptly skipped a week of school right before graduation. A group of my best friends headed to Cape Hatteras National Seashore in North Carolina for a surfing trip. The weather was warm and so was the ocean. We surfed every day and made dinner around the campfire every night. The insecure little boy who did not feel at home on that first camping trip had finally found his seat around the campfire.

Do you have a strong urge to unplug from email, social media, cable news, and digital life in general? Do you want to claim your own seat around the campfire? Then cancel your next hotel reservation and go buy yourself a tent. Decent ones can be purchased at most big-box stores for less than $100. If you are willing to spend a couple hundred dollars more, then head to a store that specializes in outdoor gear, like Cabela's, Bass Pro Shops, L.L. Bean, or REI, and you can pick up a high-quality tent that will last for years to come. Or just ask Uncle Joe if you can borrow his tent. If you don't have an Uncle Joe, then ask a friend or consider renting one online. Craigslist and Facebook Marketplace are also great places to pick up used camping gear—just beware of scammers and of meeting strangers in dark parking lots. Go with a friend. And, of course, you should make sure to inspect used gear thoroughly before purchasing it.

Tent-camping sites are very affordable. They range from $10 to $30 a night at state, county, and national parks, and from $30 and up at private campgrounds. The price of booking a tent site for a full week can easily cost less than booking a decent hotel room for a single night. Many tent sites at private campgrounds, like some in the KOA franchise system, are adding concrete pads for parking, water hookups, and, in some cases, even patio furniture and gas grills. Uncle Joe may not approve of such luxuries, but you might find your tent-camping bliss. Tent-camping sites are also widely available in desirable locations and relatively easy to reserve.

The affordability of tent camping is not the only thing that makes it attractive. Tents are also easy to buy, easy to maintain, easy to repair, and easy to transport and store. You don't need to buy an expensive new SUV or truck to go tent camping.

The barriers to entry for tent camping are low, but opportunities for great adventures are high. Feel like being alone? You can hike to tent-camping spots that are inaccessible by car or truck. Feel like falling asleep to the sound of crashing waves? You can pitch a tent in the sand just steps from the ocean. Feeling energetic? You can carry a tent to the top of a mountain and wake up above the clouds. Feel like connecting with your inner Bear Grylls? You can practice your survival and self-reliance skills by camping in the wild. Just don't eat a rhino beetle and wash it down with your own pee, okay?

Overall, tent camping is an affordable way to vacation and make memories with the folks whom you love the most. If you try it once, there is a good chance you will get hooked—just like I was. We all crave time away from the stresses of everyday life. Tent camping is an ideal way to unplug and immerse yourself in the endless wonders of the natural world.

It also should be said that, while it is easy to start tent camping, it might be hard to continue it over the long haul—or even just past age thirty. Many tent campers eventually end up desiring more comfort and convenience—things like real beds, real bathrooms, and more protection from the wind and rain. In short, many tent campers end up becoming RV owners.

Consider the following pros and cons before you spend your money on a tent that might only get used once or twice.

Pros of Tent Camping

→ Tent camping is an incredibly inexpensive way to spend a vacation. The only kind of vacation that may be cheaper probably involves sleeping in the basement of your in-laws' house. While this option is definitely less expensive than a tent-camping trip, it will take a mental toll. Trust me on this one.

→ Tent camping is an immersive experience in nature. So many of us are stressed out at work and spend too much of our free time staring at screens. Time spent in the great outdoors benefits us physically, psychologically, and even spiritually.

→ Tent camping makes us more competent and capable people. When you arrive at a tent-camping site, it is a blank canvas. After an hour or two of set up, it is your own private village, constructed with your own hands and your own creativity. Never pitched a tent or built a campfire? Tent camping will force you to master those skills, and many others, very quickly.

→ Campgrounds with tenting sites are available in almost every nook and cranny of our big, beautiful country. You can pitch a tent in your local county park or at the top of a mountain in the Rockies. Options for great tent-camping sites are everywhere. Some folks even get started right in their own backyards.

Cons of Tent Camping

→ Tent camping is dramatically affected by weather. I have spent sleepless nights in tents because of cold weather, pouring rain, and uncomfortable heat. These weather extremes have never ruined a trip for me, but they might for you, especially if you are tent camping with little kids. Unless the weather is very temperate, tent camping can require mental and physical toughness.

→ Getting a good night's sleep in a tent can be tricky, even with the right gear. Air mattresses and cots are a lot more comfortable than sleeping on the cold, hard ground, but they will never replace the comfort of an RV or cabin bed.

→ Unless you set up an incredibly elaborate camp, tenting will require you to use the toilets and showers at the campground. The quality of such facilities varies significantly from campground to campground. If you are grossed out by stepping into a shower or toilet stall that was just used by a complete stranger, then tent camping may not be for you.

→ Too much togetherness? I am all for spending quality time together in the small space of a cabin or RV, but in those places, each member of our family of five can have their own defined space. When we tent camp together, all of our stuff—and all of us—often end up in one gigantic, messy pile on the ground.

RV-Camping Adventures

About ten million Americans own RVs, and for many of them, the RV is an iconic symbol of freedom and the open road. It certainly is for us.

As a youngish couple with energetic twin boys, we found ourselves buried under diapers and endless household chores. We were sleep deprived and mentally and physically exhausted. We wanted to breathe fresh air again and get out on the open road. So we did.

We bought our first RV because we wanted a magic memory machine. We wanted to give our children the type of childhood that neither of us had. I also thought that it might spark a new, more romantic chapter in our marriage and make us feel young and carefree again. Realistic expectations, right?

Our first trip to a state park in South Jersey was almost a complete disaster. When we pulled into the campground (with mini cribs strapped to the roof racks of our Toyota), we discovered that the battery cover had blown off of the camper. Then I started to set the camper up and realized that I didn't really remember how to do it. Our salesman had promised me that I could set it up in less than fifteen minutes. He even showed me how to do it. Apparently the lesson didn't stick.

An hour later, I was sweating and grunting and swatting away Max and Theo, who seemed to be doing high-speed loops around my legs. Eventually, I raised the camper roof and pulled out the bed ends and...we were camping!

I felt like an early American settler raising the roof on his first home somewhere out in the Wild West. I felt triumphant. But the feeling didn't last long. Before I knew it, the boys were running us both ragged. We spent the next few hours retrieving them from the woods and depositing them back on our site, again and again. They never sat still. Even for a second. Back then, taking them camping was exhausting. But as Stephanie liked to point out, so was staying at home.

Tips for Your First RV Trip

- ✧ Practice backing up and parking the RV before your first trip.
- ✧ Practice using all the systems (heat, AC, plumbing, slide-outs, etc.) at home.
- ✧ Practice hitching and unhitching at home.
- ✧ Camp close to home for an initial shakedown trip.
- ✧ Reserve a site at a private campground first. State and county parks can be harder to navigate with no one around to help.
- ✧ Reserve a pull-through site (so you don't have to back in).
- ✧ Avoid driving at night, if possible.
- ✧ Don't be afraid to ask other RV owners for help.
- ✧ Keep the first trip simple, and plan plenty of time in and around the RV as you get used to it.
- ✧ Keep your sense of humor. Stuff happens and things break. That's okay.

Eventually we put those babies to bed. Then something magical happened. We stepped outside the RV and built a crackling campfire. Stephanie poured herself a glass of wine, and we pulled our chairs closer together. We laughed about how utterly unprepared we were as RV owners—and as parents. We talked about the kids, and we talked about each other. It felt like date night in the great outdoors.

Our pop-up camper was hard to set up that first time, but it was also comfortable and convenient. We had a toilet and running water. We could take hot showers and cook inside, and we had comfortable beds and plenty of space for our family.

It took us hours to set up and break down that weekend. But on the drive home, we were both laughing and planning our next trip while the boys snoozed in the back seat. We had spent time with the kids and with each other, and we'd packed it all into one crazy weekend. What was not to love? It was a heck of a lot better than watching *Top Chef* in a hotel bathroom, that's for sure.

We fell head over heels in love with RVing on that trip. That pop-up camper took us to Cape Hatteras for surfing trips, to the Blue Ridge Mountains for bluegrass music, and to Acadia National Park for hiking and lobster rolls. We spent twenty nights camping during that first season. Then thirty nights the next season. Setting up and breaking down the pop-up camper eventually got tiring, so we upgraded to a fancier travel trailer with a bunkhouse. Thank goodness, because our third son, Wes, was born soon after.

RV ownership has changed our lives for the better and brought our family closer together. When my three boys face challenges in their lives, I hope they will look back at our RV adventures and find deep reserves of happiness and joy. I know that I do.

Do you have a burning desire to escape into the great outdoors but want all the comforts of home while you travel? Then you should seriously consider RV ownership. Owning an RV is like owning a vacation home you can take anywhere. I may never own a beach house or a cabin in the mountains, but I can take my RV to both places. In fact, we often do so on the same trip.

There are excellent campgrounds in every state and in almost every tourist destination in the country. If you want to visit our national parks, you can do so in an RV. If you want to visit our cities and urban destinations, you can do so in an RV. Even large cities like New York City and San Francisco have nearby options for RV owners.

American campgrounds offer a breathtaking variety of experiences, from rustic to resort, and at much lower price points than hotels or cruises. RV ownership is also more affordable than you might think. You can easily buy a decent used pop-up camper for $1,000 on Craigslist or Facebook Marketplace or purchase a new travel trailer for $10,000 at a reputable RV dealership. You can also spend $75,000 to $500,000 on a new motorhome, if you have the budget and inclination. There is an RV for everyone at every price point. The most important thing to remember is that the family in a used pop-up camper is having just as much fun as the family in an expensive motorhome. The family in the brand-new motorhome may be more comfortable than the family in the well-used pop-up camper, but having fun and being comfortable are two very different things. Of that I am certain.

Pros of RV Camping

-» RV vacations are affordable. In our personal experience, they cost about half as much as a vacation in a hotel or motel.

-» RVs provide all of the comforts of home, including your own bed, your own bathroom, and your own kitchen.

-» RVs increase the comfort of travel. When we pull into rest stops, we can avoid overpriced fast food and prepare meals in our own kitchen. We can also avoid crowded and unsanitary rest-stop bathrooms by using our own bathroom.

-» You can bring your own stuff. We like to travel with small things like our own food and our own bedding, as well as large things like bikes, kayaks, and outdoor cooking equipment. Our RV lets us bring it all.

-» Your dog can come along. Pet-friendly hotels can be hard to come by, but pet-friendly campgrounds are everywhere.

Cons of RV Camping

→ If you check into a hotel room and the heat or AC isn't working, the hotel is responsible for fixing it. If you show up at a campground and your RV is not working, it is your responsibility to fix it. This can add stress to a vacation, particularly if you are not handy or if you are camping in the middle of nowhere without a dealer or mobile repairman nearby.

→ RVs depreciate in value more rapidly than cars and trucks. If you borrow too much money to buy one, you could easily end up owing the bank more money than it's worth.

→ RVs require maintenance and upkeep. Maintaining a motorhome is far more expensive than maintaining a towable RV—but there are annual expenses and upkeep for each.

→ If you really like staying directly downtown in cities, and not on the outskirts or in a nearby suburb, then an RV will probably not be able to get you there. Driving a motorhome or towable RV through a city can also be stressful and difficult.

Cabin-Camping Adventures

After seven years of RVing, I had begrudgingly accepted the fact that certain bucket-list trips would have to wait until later in life. We often daydreamed about taking a trip to the Pacific Northwest, but the idea of driving sixty hours with three rambunctious boys in the back seat of our pickup truck sounded like a nightmare. Stephanie and I could hike the snow-capped mountains of Olympic National Park and gaze up at towering redwoods once the boys were all in college.

I wanted every trip to be an RV trip, but this desire was causing me to draw some restrictive geographical boundaries around my dreams. Thankfully, Stephanie had other plans.

She wanted to leave our RV at home and go on a cabin-camping trip in the Pacific Northwest. At first I resisted. I was so completely in love with the RV lifestyle that I couldn't imagine leaving our trailer at home. But then she showed me the cabins and accommodations she was researching in Washington, Oregon, and Northern California. They were all gorgeous—and they were all at campgrounds. She convinced me that as long as we stayed at campgrounds, and not hotels, it would still be the dream trip we had always imagined. She was right.

We ended up loving cabin camping every bit as much as traveling in our RV. That twenty-seven-day trip to the Pacific Northwest was our greatest family adventure...so far. It was everything a dream trip should be. We stayed in a rental house just outside Olympic National Park, a cabin on a lake at the base of Mount St. Helens, a glamping tent right on the beach in Oregon, a deluxe cabin just steps away from an old-growth redwood forest, and a log cabin on a stunning lake in central Oregon. Every stop was at a campground. No hotels in sight.

---------- **Tips for Your First Cabin-Camping Trip** ----------

⬦ Carefully research all the cabin options at a campground, and pick a cabin model that is a good fit for your family.

⬦ Make sure to consider the cancellation policies before booking. Some campgrounds will not return deposits, and this can be surprising to new campers.

⬦ Inquire about linens and towel supplies. You may want to bring some extra blankets even if linens are provided.

⬦ Find out what kitchen supplies are stocked.

⬦ Bring your tent-camping kitchen and pantry supplies just in case, if you have them. We always pack ours to ensure that we have paper towels, tinfoil, a bottle opener, and other random items.

We hiked up snow-capped mountains on Hurricane Ridge in Olympic National Park, climbed atop fallen redwoods in Northern California, and slept just a few yards away from crashing waves on the Oregon coast. We descended—with lanterns and jackets—into the lava tubes beneath Mount St. Helens, drank coffee at Pike Place Market in Seattle, and spent hours reading at Powell's Books in Portland. We did all of these things with three young boys by our side. We didn't wait until we were older and had the time and inclination to make the cross-country drive without them. We followed our bliss by staying at campgrounds. And we had an unforgettable adventure that was perfectly suited for our family.

Cabin camping offered us so many of the same things that we loved about RVing. We were able to cook our own food instead of eating out every meal, and we ended every day with a campfire. Each cabin rental also allowed us to experience the great outdoors in ways that a hotel room could never do. We just had to step outside the front door to immerse ourselves in the natural beauty of the Pacific Northwest.

Do you really want to try a campground vacation but find the thought of tent camping too daunting? Does RV ownership sound intriguing, but you don't have enough vacation time to justify the expense? Then a cabin-camping trip may be perfect for you. Renting a cabin gives you all of the benefits of the campground experience without having to buy a tent or an RV. Plus, cabins are super cute and super cozy.

A cabin vacation may cost just as much as a hotel vacation, but we think that you get more bang for your buck. Generally speaking, a cabin with a kitchen and bathroom costs about as much as a nice hotel room in the same area, but it has at least twice the space. Each of our cabins in Washington, Oregon, and California had bunks for the kids, full kitchens, and outdoor patio space—plus a front yard with a picnic table and firepit.

--- **Six Unique Campground Accommodations Worth Trying** ---

1. Astronomy lodge with private observation deck and telescope (Herkimer Diamond Mines KOA Resort, Herkimer County, New York)
2. Seaside shanties (Oceanside RV Resort & Campground, Coos Bay, Oregon)
3. Caboose rental (Lake-In-Wood Camping Resort, Lancaster County, Pennsylvania)
4. Mountain-view treetop cabins (Yogi Bear's Jellystone Park, Golden Valley, North Carolina)
5. Airstream rentals (Flying Flags RV Resort & Campground, Santa Barbara County, California)
6. Vintage trailer rentals (Enchanted Trails RV Park & Trading Post, Albuquerque, New Mexico)

When you rent a hotel room, you are reserving a small interior space. When you rent a cabin, you get more interior space...and your own outdoor space. Plus, there is no one sleeping above you, below you, and on both sides of you. If you are traveling with several kids, you should easily be able to find a cabin with a dedicated bed for each of them and, more often than not, a separate, private bedroom for Mom and Dad. Renting a larger cabin is really equivalent to paying for two hotel rooms, and how many families can afford that?

Staying in one hotel room is always a claustrophobic squeeze for our family, but cabins can provide more privacy and some much-needed room to stretch our legs. Many campgrounds also offer pet-friendly cabins, so your beloved pup can come too.

If you decide to rent a cabin for an upcoming adventure, make sure to ask what is provided, such as linens and towels, and what things you may have to bring, like coffee and filters. Showing up without linens at a cabin that does not provide them can ruin a vacation. The only thing worse would be waking up and discovering that the campground provided a coffee machine—but did not provide filters!

Actually, the only thing worse for us is waking up in a hotel room. So we try to avoid them as much as we can.

Pros of Cabin Camping

→ When you have a problem with a broken tent or RV, it is your job to fix it. But when you rent a cabin, the campground is responsible for making sure everything is working right— and if it's not, it's their job to fix it. This simple shift in dynamic can make your vacation far less stressful and unpredictable.

→ Cabin camping should require significantly less gear than tent camping or RVing.

-⤛ Cabins are great for rainy days. They have lots of room for board games and plenty of comfortable seating for reading or watching movies.

-⤛ RVs have long-term maintenance costs. Cabin rentals do not—at least not for the consumer.

Cons of Cabin Camping

-⤛ Cabin rentals cost significantly more than tent-camping sites and RV sites.

-⤛ Many cabin rentals have strict cancellation policies and require large deposits to secure.

-⤛ Many campgrounds only have a few cabin rental options and some have no cabin rental options at all.

-⤛ The comfort of the beds and furniture in a cabin rental is very unpredictable. Picky sleepers beware.

♯

Last year we finally bought a tent, some good sleeping bags, and cots for the kids. Why, you might ask? Because Stephanie didn't want the boys to get soft—and neither did I. During our first family tent-camping trip, Wes woke up in the middle of the night. He was crying. So I stumbled out of bed and grabbed a flashlight.

"Gotta go potty, dude?"

"Yes, Daddy."

"Let's go."

He stopped crying.

Wes and I carefully stepped over the familiar bodies snoozing away in their warm sleeping bags, so as not to wake them up. Then I fumbled around with the zipper and unzipped the tent. We stepped outside together into the crisp night air. Without thinking, I turned my flashlight on and grabbed his tiny hand. We walked down a slight embankment toward a patch of thick bushes right next to a gurgling stream—the same stream that had lulled us all to sleep a few hours before.

Then we both dropped our drawers and peed together under the stars. One minute he was standing next to me. But the next minute I noticed he was gone from my side. He didn't need me to guide him back to our tent. When I turned around, he was already halfway there.

F or the first few years of our family camping journey, we truly thought the RV was the reason we were having so much fun. It took a bucket-list trip to the Pacific Northwest to teach us a very valuable lesson. It wasn't really about the RV...it was about the campground.

For our family, the campground environment makes travel enjoyable instead of daunting and stressful. Whether we are visiting a national park or a major city, being able to decompress at the end of the day by riding bikes or sitting around a campfire is the secret formula for us. So many things are different about the campground versus the hotel experience. In the mornings, we can enjoy breakfast in our pajamas around a picnic table rather than a hotel lobby or restaurant. In the afternoons, us parents can lay in a hammock and read while the kids play catch. And at night, we can gaze at the stars instead of a TV screen.

Realizing that we could have all these perks even if we weren't traveling in our own personal RV was nothing short of a revelation for us as we planned future family trips. After that visit to the PNW, we spent the next spring break cabin camping in Texas. In the mornings, we explored San Antonio, Hill Country, Austin, and the Fort Worth Stockyards. In the afternoons, the kids went down waterslides and played laser tag at the campgrounds. Our boys sometimes claim that this was their favorite camping trip ever, although the list changes according to their moods.

Discovering the value of cabin camping wasn't our only aha moment after years of traveling in our personal RV. We also dipped our toes into the world of RV rentals, and we've now had quite a few amazing adventures in rented campers as well.

Our very first experience with an RV rental was, of all places, at Disney World. Jeremy and I had to fly down to Florida in the middle of winter for work. He decided that it would be a dream to combine the business trip with a family vacation to Disney World. There was only one problem: the very idea of Disney World gave me heartburn.

I'd had one very unmagical childhood trip to Disney, and I wasn't at all eager for a repeat experience. Jeremy, on the other hand, was determined to be a living, breathing Disney Dad. Throughout Jeremy's difficult childhood years, his grandfather had repeatedly swept him away on amazing Disney vacations with his cousins. They would stay in suites at the Contemporary Resort, ride Space Mountain thirty times in a row, and charge massive ice-cream sundaes to the hotel room. In contrast, my own memories from my one semidisastrous visit mostly include my father complaining loudly about how dang expensive and crowded the place was.

The carrot that Jeremy dangled in front of me to get me to agree to the trip was Fort Wilderness, the resort campground that is actually on Disney World property. He convinced me that this would be just another camping trip with a few low-key jaunts into the theme parks. It was a decent compromise. I bit and we booked.

The thought of driving twenty hours to get to "the Happiest Place on Earth" did not appeal to either of us, especially during the winter when inclement weather could make towing an RV dicey at best. Plus, airline tickets from New York City to Orlando are actually cheaper than driving when you calculate the price of gas and tolls. So we decided to try renting an RV. We boarded an airplane with our three boys for the very first time in their lives. After our business event, we all headed to Disney World in a Class C

RV rental that we picked up near the airport. Jeremy drove the motorhome to Disney, and I drove it back to the airport. We both loved driving it and felt comfortable doing so almost immediately.

Staying in a rental RV for five nights in Fort Wilderness turned me into a Disney convert. Everyone I ever knew came back from Disney World exhausted and wrung out. We, on the other hand, enjoyed a pretty relaxing family vacation. We headed into the parks early in the morning and returned to the campground by late afternoon, so we could chill around the pool. Then we grilled hamburgers at the campsite and walked to the nightly Chip 'n' Dale's Campfire Sing-A-Long. We toasted s'mores and went "looping"—the Fort Wilderness tradition of driving your golf cart around the campground and enjoying the decorated RVs. I was completely smitten, and Jeremy had no trouble convincing me to return to Disney the following year, when work again called us to Florida. It was a no-brainer for us to rent another RV and camp at Fort Wilderness.

I wonder if there is any place where the magic of the campground came into clearer focus for me than Fort Wilderness at Disney World. Even though we stood in line for rides and fought crowds to get a view of the parades just like everyone else, our days were bookended by natural beauty and outdoor fun. In the morning, Jeremy and I could quietly drink our coffee while our boys played tetherball and basketball on the campground loop. Wild turkeys and deer would wander through the campsite in the evenings. We could walk down to the stables for some pony rides or take a hike on one of the beautiful trails. I know for certain that this decompression time made it possible for me to enjoy all the frenetic fun of the parks.

Real-World Costs for Renting an RV

Fort Wilderness (Five Nights)

Cost of campsite at Fort Wilderness, premier red carpet: $800

Cost of RV rental, including delivery, set up, and breakdown; fully stocked with bedding, linens, and cooking supplies; plus golf-cart rental: $1,380

Total for accommodations: $2,180

When we crunch the numbers, it doesn't necessarily come out cheaper to rent an RV and camp at Fort Wilderness than it is to stay in one of the budget resorts at Disney. In fact, we probably break even on costs compared to resorts like Pop Century or Art of Animation. But camping isn't just about the economic value for our family. It's about the overall experience. I wouldn't have traded the peace and quiet of the evenings at Fort Wilderness for a chance to stay at one of the luxury Disney resorts. Seriously.

⌗

Back when we bought our first pop-up trailer, the option of renting an RV instead of buying one was not on our radar. At the time, there were just a couple of big corporate RV rental operations in business, like Cruise America and Road Bear RV. Their advertising certainly wasn't reaching our segment of the marketplace. If anything, their target audience was European families coming over to the United States for epic, cross-country vacations. And even if we had researched renting an RV, I'm pretty sure we wouldn't have bitten. The price tags from those large rental corporations can be pretty daunting. At the time, we didn't understand the value packed into an RV rental, so spending more than $300 per night would have seemed crazy to us. But then came the world of peer-to-peer RV rentals and nothing was ever the same.

Who Is Renting RVs?

Among all campers who say they primarily camp in RVs, 44 percent do not own the RV they use the most. Some borrow an RV from someone they know, and others rent from traditional RV rental companies or peer-to-peer rental services.

(KOA, 2018 North American Camping Report)

At some point in the last five years or so, a few creative entrepreneurs realized that there were a lot of RVs sitting unused in people's driveways for the majority of the year. Why wouldn't owners want to make money renting out their RV when they couldn't use it themselves? They basically took the Airbnb concept and applied it to the world of RVs. Fast-forward to the present day, and peer-to-peer RV renting is a thriving marketplace. The largest platforms, like Outdoorsy and RVshare, have thousands of rental options, ranging from $50-per-night pop-up campers to $350-per-night motorhomes.

Family RV, Cabin Camping, or RV Rental?

When we bought our first RV, I think we imagined that we would never travel any other way again. Years later, we realized that we really *did* want to visit San Francisco, but we really *didn't* want to spend four days getting there and four days getting home. Not every trip has to be a cross-country road-trip adventure. Peer-to-peer RV rentals have opened up a whole new world of possibility for our family and other people like us who simply prefer campgrounds to hotels.

We now enjoy the freedom of choosing any vacation destination, no matter how far away it is, and the excitement of researching all the RV rental options in that area. We look into corporate rentals, dealerships, and peer-to-peer options. We check out available rigs and compare prices. Some of our friends have even rented RVs when traveling abroad in places like Germany, England, New Zealand, and Iceland. Hearing about their amazing experiences has definitely made international travel with our kids seem more accessible and appealing.

So how have we decided when to rent an RV and when to stay in a cabin? The destinations have mostly made this decision for us. When we were traveling to the Pacific Northwest, there were fully stocked luxury cabin options in every destination we wished to visit.

- - - - - - - - - - - -   Real-World Costs for Renting an RV   - - - - - - - - - - - -

South Dakota Road Trip (Nine Nights)

Cost of RV rental: $1,125

Cost of campsites: $420

Total for accommodations: $1,545

South Dakota, however, was an entirely different sort of trip. We very much wanted to stay at the rustic campgrounds in Badlands National Park and Custer State Park. Some of these places are legendary among RVers, and we wanted that authentic experience. Since fully stocked cabins were not available at all of our planned stops, we rented an RV for the trip.

In recent months, we've been planning a trip to Glacier National Park and have found that there are virtually no peer-to-peer rental options in that remote area, so we've already booked cabins on both the east and west sides of the park. The cabins come with linens, towels, and fully stocked kitchens, so they work perfectly for our family. One thing we've learned through our experiences is to *never* rent a rustic cabin when flying to a destination. I had to pack blankets, pillows, and towels on a flight to Florida one time and vowed to never make that mistake again.

The bottom line is that we have so many great options on the table when we are planning our next family adventure. If we can get to the destination in one or two driving days, then we'll embrace the opportunity to travel in our personal RV. However, for farther destinations, we'll seek out affordable and accessible rental options or cabin-camping options.

The RV and camping industries have exploded in growth since we bought our first pop-up camper. At the time, campgrounds weren't offering the range of accommodations that are available now, like deluxe cabins and glamping tents, and there weren't these large peer-to-peer marketplaces that connect RV owners with potential renters. But now that they're here, we're determined to take full advantage of all these benefits for folks like us who just want to end every traveling day at the campground.

RV rentals have already given us some pretty amazing family memories. We can't wait to see what the next experience brings.

Important Things to Keep in Mind about Renting an RV

→ *Be prepared for a steep learning curve.* If this is your first rental, you'll have to learn quite a bit to operate the unit. It's a house on wheels, after all. RVs have heating systems, sewer systems, and water heaters. Some have generators and convertors. It gets so much easier with practice, but the first rental experience can be overwhelming.

→ *It's not usually cheaper than staying in a hotel or Airbnb.* Oftentimes the cost of a campsite plus the rental will equal the cost of a budget hotel. Renting an RV should be more about the experience than a cost-saving measure.

→ *There's a wide range of price points and quality.* You'll find old pop-up campers for $50 per night and brand-new motorhomes for $350 per night. Pick one that matches the experience you wish to have.

→ *Pay attention to what is included in a rental.* Some will include linens and bedding, but some won't. You probably don't want to provide your own cups, utensils, and coffee maker. I've learned this the hard way, and now I specifically look for rentals that include everything. The South Dakota rental even had paper towels and all-purpose cleaning spray. It was fabulous.

---

5 Great Reasons to Rent an RV

1. You are considering buying an RV and want to try the experience first.
2. You want to buy an RV but are unsure of which type.
3. You want to vacation with friends or family that already own an RV.
4. You love traveling by RV but won't be able to travel enough to justify the investment of purchasing one.
5. You want to maximize vacation time and minimize traveling time by flying and renting an RV.

↟ *Read the reviews carefully.* Some rental companies provide concierge service, walking you through every step of the process and even providing vacation-planning support. Some owners seem to leave renters to fend for themselves.

↟ *Look for detailed information about insurance and roadside assistance.* The best rental companies have all the legal work done for you. Beware of renting privately off of Craigslist and not being covered in case of an accident.

↟ *Some rentals are pet friendly and some are not.* If you want to travel with your furry family members, make sure to track down a pet-friendly rental. This is one of the best perks of RV travel, but don't assume that all rentals will welcome Fido. Our South Dakota rental wasn't listed as pet friendly, but we contacted the owner and vouched for our sweet Maggie. The owner was happy to let us bring her along.

Recommended RV Rental Options

↟ **Cruise America:** This company has been around since the 1970s and is a great option for folks who want to be baby-stepped through an RV rental. The rigs are simple and basic, designed to streamline the renter experience. They have 130 locations around the country. You'll pay a higher price with Cruise America, but you'll get concierge service.

↟ **Road Bear RV:** This is another rental company that has been around for decades, and they also have customer service dialed in. Road Bear RV only has seven locations, but they are near major American cities like New York City, Denver, and Los Angeles. You'll pay a premium and receive a lot of support in planning your rental adventure.

- ⟶ **Outdoorsy:** Outdoorsy is a peer-to-peer RV rental service, connecting RV owners in the United States and Canada with potential renters. You'll find RV options of every class and size. You'll also find a wide variety of price points. Outdoorsy does background checks on renters and provides liability insurance policies of up to $1 million, giving peace of mind to both parties. You can also pay extra for emergency roadside assistance.

- ⟶ **RVshare:** RVshare is similar to the Outdoorsy model, with thousands of privately owned RVs available for rent throughout the United States. They also offer insurance and twenty-four-hour roadside assistance. The website is very user friendly and offers a ton of resources for first-time renters.

- ⟶ **RV rental outfitters:** A variety of private companies provide rental services near major American destinations like Glacier National Park, Yellowstone, and Yosemite. Many of these companies have been operating for years and provide everything you need to have an adventurous camping experience in bucket-list locations. Some will even book campgrounds and excursions for you. We've used one of these services for Disney, and the company delivered the camper, set up the campsite, and included a free golf cart.

- ⟶ **Local dealerships:** Many RV dealerships maintain a fleet of RV rentals. Sometimes they provide optional kitchen and linen kits for an extra fee, but we have found dealer rentals to be not as well stocked in general. This might be a better option for folks looking to rent near their home base.

Tips for First-Time Renters

→ **Don't go too big or too complicated.** An RV is a house on wheels, and learning everything at once can be overwhelming.

→ **Consider renting a motorized RV rather than a towable RV.** Small motorized RVs like Class Bs and Class Cs can be as easy to drive as vans and U-Haul trucks.

→ **Watch YouTube videos in advance.** You can find videos on driving, setting up, and operating a wide array of RVs. Use these as a resource for getting more comfortable before you get behind the wheel

→ **Join camping groups on social media for tips on planning.** RVers love sharing their favorite campgrounds and road-trip expertise.

→ **Get detailed lists of what is included in the rental.** This includes linens, bedding, kitchen supplies, camp chairs, toilet paper, etc.

→ **Don't go too far from home or plan too much traveling per day.** RVing has a steep learning curve, and keeping it simple will keep things stress-free and enjoyable.

→ **Get written instructions for all the RV systems.** This includes directions for turning on the water heater, using the propane, and emptying the holding tanks. Many rental companies and owners provide videos as well.

→ **Have a sense of humor and enjoy the adventure.** Renting an RV might be one of the most memorable family travel experiences you ever have. But stepping outside of the box can bring unexpected challenges. Go with the flow and have fun.

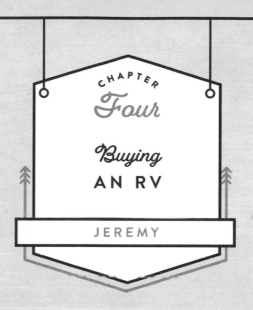

After that fifteen-hour marathon drive to Asheville when the boys took turns crying for the duration of the trip, and then the disastrous weekend at the CoCo Key Water Resort (see Chapter One), Stephanie and I knew we had to find a different way to travel as a family.

She had mentioned buying a pop-up camper a few times over the course of our marriage—but to be honest, it kind of went in one ear and out the other. But now, after our epic "vacation" with the in-laws and our CoCo Key weekend "getaway," I was finally open to listening more carefully.

Then I saw a Go RVing commercial while I was watching a baseball game. It featured a father and his sons camping alongside a crystal-clear stream in a pop-up camper. This thirty-second commercial hit all of the right sentimental notes for me. It was exactly what I wanted for my family. Adventurous road trips? Check! Family time in the great outdoors? Check!

Now that Stephanie had me on board, she handed off the research to me. I would have to do the dirty work. When it comes to money, I often do the dirty work—in more ways than one.

My initial research was encouraging, and soon I was completely hooked. RV ownership seemed affordable for a family operating on two teachers' salaries. Campsites at state and national parks only cost about $20 to $30 per night, and private campgrounds with more amenities only cost about $40 to $80 dollars per night. A decent hotel room for our family in the same locations could easily cost three times that...and the four of us would be sharing beds in a tightly packed room.

The idea of having our own beds and kitchen while traveling was also mighty appealing to both of us. Max and Theo could bring along their teddy bears, blankets, and pillows, and we would all have a familiar and comfortable place to sleep each night. We wouldn't have to hear noisy strangers through the walls next to us, and we wouldn't have to worry about our boys waking up Stephanie's parents on our next trip to Asheville. We could just camp nearby.

So we loaded the boys up on a snowy Saturday morning and headed to Stone's Camping World in South Jersey to look at used pop-up campers.

But why were we fixated on pop-up campers and not some other type of RV? Simple: because we had not taken the time to educate ourselves about all of our options. There were also some powerful emotions at work. When Stephanie and I were little kids, pop-up campers were hugely popular, and many of the middle-class families we knew owned them. Neither of ours ever did. I think this created a sense of longing in both of us for what might have been.

So I think it's fair to say that we were hell-bent on righting some generational wrongs. Were we being a bit grandiose and a bit idealistic? Perhaps.

But grandiosity and idealism are the absolute right of every sleep-deprived parent who is knee-deep in diapers and dirty laundry. In fact, in some cases, they are the only things that keep young parents going.

We planned on starting our RV journey with $3,000 that we had squirreled away from our teaching salaries. The guiding idea was to purchase our dream machine with cash. Initially, we had no plans to take out a loan. But that $3,000 budget quickly turned into a down payment on a $12,000 pop-up camper. Why? Because dreams can't be purchased on the cheap, can they? Or maybe it was just because our salesman was really, really good.

Stephanie and I are both tough negotiators, but we were putty in this guy's hands. He was super slick and wore tight black jeans and cowboy boots. He knew he wasn't selling us an RV...he was selling us freedom and liberation from those dirty diapers and laundry. He walked us right past a handful of used pop-ups that they had on the lot because, as he put it, *"Those are not for you!"* When he wasn't talking his sweet talk, he was whistling "Midnight Rider."

Then he walked us into a shiny new pop-up camper with a shower, toilet, stereo (with auxiliary jack!), heated beds, and an electric lifter system. I felt like a prince surveying his future kingdom. I only had to plunk down a $3K deposit and sign a few papers to claim it as my own. When I looked at Stephanie, I could tell that she was also impressed with all of the comfort and convenience. This was no army-issued canvas tent! To say that we were both completely sold would be an understatement. For us, it was a brand-new pop-up camper or bust! We would own it for the next few decades and show our kids the beauty of America.

So we borrowed the money and bought it. It was the best—and worst—decision that we have ever made.

It was the best decision because it turned our family into a camping family and introduced us to the RV lifestyle. It was the worst decision because we spent *way* too much money, and a pop-up was not really the right RV for the way our family ended up traveling. Of course, we didn't know that yet. But we hadn't spent much time thinking about it either. We should have either stuck with the idea of buying a used pop-up camper, or we should have done more research and bought an entry-level travel trailer for the same price. Shoulda. Woulda. Coulda.

What we did do was fall head over heels in love with camping. Max and Theo loved it too. Their faces lit up every time we hitched up and headed out. We all loved it so much that we started to go a lot. Almost every other weekend. Then we started to take longer trips in the summer. When we bought the rig, we figured that we would camp a few weekends a year and take a weeklong family vacation each summer. But we ended up camping more than thirty nights a year by our second season.

The bonds in our extended families continued to strain under the pressure of geography, politics, religion, and financial issues—but our immediate family unit finally began to make sense to us. In fact, that time spent together at the campground helped us find and forge our own identity as a family. We were stubbornly refusing to fritter our lives away worrying about details. The campground was like our Walden Pond. But with a playground and full hookups.

It quickly became obvious that the entire camping lifestyle was perfect for us, but it also became obvious that the pop-up camper was not. Setting it up and breaking it down again and again on trips with multiple stops was beginning to wear us all down. So after two summers, we decided to trade in the pop-up camper as fast as we could. We wanted the travel trailer that we probably should have bought in the first place.

Unfortunately, we owed more on the pop-up camper than it was worth. This is common when you buy an RV with a small down payment and a long-term loan, particularly if you trade it in too quickly. Just like with an auto loan, the early payments are almost entirely interest. RV values also depreciate more quickly than car and truck values. We were about $2,000 underwater when we showed up at the dealership on that fateful day. But I had recently won a $10,000 teacher-of-the-year award at my school. Thankfully, we had the cash to cover that loss and we were able to make a 50 percent down payment on the new RV. Our monthly payment would stay about the same. Live and learn, right?

Like so many first-time RV owners, we thought we would own our pop-up camper for a decade, and we ended up trading it in after two seasons. You see, an awful lot of RVers start out with a pop-up camper, fall in love with camping, and then move into travel trailers very quickly. It is pretty much a joke among experienced owners, hence the famous saying, "Buy your second RV first."

When we bought our second RV, we knew exactly what we wanted (a travel trailer) and how much we should spend on it. We owned our Jayco White Hawk 29SQB travel trailer for the next six years and spent hundreds of nights in it. It was the perfect RV for our family. It was easy to set up and easy to break down, and there was plenty of room for Wes when he was born a year after we bought it.

Hopefully we can help you avoid making the same mistakes we did when we bought our first RV—and make the learning curve a little less steep. Hopefully you can buy your second RV first, or at least not overspend like we did.

Your Journey Toward RV Ownership

On your journey toward RV ownership, the first thing you need to know is that there is an RV at every price point. It sounds like a well-crafted piece of industry propaganda, but it's true. If you are willing to buy a used pop-up camper or travel trailer, you can find decent options for around $1K to $5K. If you want something new in the same broad category, $8K to $20K can easily make it happen. If you have more than $20K to spend, things get nice pretty fast. Are you rolling with more than $50K to spend? You might start thinking about a motorhome.

There is also an RV for every different type of camping style. Are you the rugged, outdoorsy type? There are dozens of RVs specifically designed for off-grid adventures. More interested in feeling like your RV is a luxurious vacation home? No problem. Plenty of new RVs come with stainless-steel appliances, reclining couches, flat-screen TVs, and many other residential design features. There are also hundreds of options in between rugged and luxurious. But here's the bad news: you can only buy one RV at a time, and choosing can be pretty overwhelming.

Do you want to find that perfect RV on your first attempt and avoid quickly trading up like we did? Do you want to buy your second RV first? Well, the first thing you have to do is narrow down the RV type (or class) that will work best for your needs. In other words, you need to do what we didn't do! Here are five questions you should ask that will help you decide which RV type should be on your short list. After this list of important questions, we will give you a quick breakdown of each RV type, along with some pros and cons.

 What's your price range?

Okay, in a perfect world there would be no budgets, right? Unfortunately, money matters, and we all have a general idea of how much we can afford to spend on an RV purchase. Once you have settled on a comfortable shopping budget, it will be much easier to narrow down your options and focus on the rigs that are in the running for your first purchase. Please remember that just because you *can* borrow a lot of money to buy an RV doesn't mean you *should* borrow a lot of money to buy one. Borrowing a lot of money to purchase a depreciating asset is a recipe for financial pain. If you do borrow money to buy an RV, try to aim for a monthly payment that looks like your cable bill or car payment, not your mortgage.

2 **What is your current tow vehicle situation?** This is important! If you currently have a truck or SUV that can tow an RV, you are in good shape to buy a folding camping trailer, travel trailer, or maybe even a fifth wheel. But make sure to check how much weight your vehicle can tow before buying the RV. Use the VIN number to get an accurate figure. The same automobile model can have a wide variety of towing capacities because of

optional packages. Don't take a salesman's word on the tow capacity of your vehicle—it is ultimately your responsibility to know the numbers. The salesman is not responsible for the safety of your family. Only you are.

If you don't already own a potential tow vehicle, carefully consider a motorized RV purchase. The price of a tow vehicle plus a towable RV can easily be equal to the price of a Class C motorhome or an entry-level Class A. There's no reason to give up that great commuter car if you don't want to!

3 **Who will be traveling in the RV?** Some folks shop for an RV thinking about anyone and everyone who might, at some point, join them on their travels. It's a good idea to focus on shopping for the people (and pets) who will be in the RV *most* of the time. If you're thinking about towable RVs, would everyone in the family have a comfortable seat in the tow vehicle? If you're looking at motorized

RVs, make sure there are seat belts for all travelers and think about where you would place necessary car seats.

4 **Are you a road-tripper, destination traveler, or seasonal camper?** We tend to be road-trippers, heading out for weeks at a time and visiting lots of different locations. This means that we like an RV that is pretty easy to hitch and unhitch. We also don't want to worry too much about height restrictions when traveling around our native northeastern region. Some folks, however, love to take their RVs to just one amazing spot and set up camp for a weeklong vacation. For them, a spacious fifth wheel might fit the bill. Traveling in more urban places? Check out Class Bs. Want to cover a lot of distance in comfort and style? Class Cs or As are often perfect cross-country options.

5 **Do you prefer private or public campgrounds?** If you are new to RVing, this may be a tricky question to answer, but here is a quick tutorial (with more to come in Chapter Five). In general, public campgrounds tend to be more rustic and beautiful, but they also tend to be older and less modernized. So if you know you want to stay in state and national parks, make sure you don't purchase an RV that is too big for the majority of the campsites. The rule of thumb is to stay under thirty feet if you want to camp mostly in public campgrounds.

On the other hand, private campgrounds often offer pull-through campsites that can accommodate rigs up to forty feet long. So if you know you prefer modern amenities and full hookups, go ahead and get that larger fifth wheel or Class A.

When you imagine your RV dream, what does it look like? Are you escaping from the city and heading for off-grid adventures? Maybe you're driving all over this beautiful country, exploring urban destinations and national parks. No matter what your RV dream is, there's a rig that will be perfect for it.

Which RV Is Right for Me?

Now that you have asked yourself the previous five questions, you should be better equipped to pick the right first RV for your family. Here is a quick breakdown of each major type of RV and some pros and cons for each.

Pop-Up Campers (a.k.a. Tent Trailers or Camping Trailers)

Pop-up campers are towable RVs that fold down into relatively small and low-profile packages. The beds pull out and the unit is enclosed with durable canvas walls. Our pop-up camper was not right for us, but, ironically, we really missed it after we traded it in. Sleeping with the screened windows open during a cool fall night is just like heaven.

Pros of a Pop-Up Camper

▷ lightweight and easy to tow

▷ budget friendly and easy to store

▷ very comfortable sleeping arrangements and plenty of beds

▷ screened windows allow for an immersive natural experience

▷ great for single-destination trips because of extensive set up

▷ many used units for sale on Craigslist and Facebook Marketplace

Cons of a Pop-Up Camper

▷ canvas maintenance

▷ condensation issues related to the canvas

▷ more moving parts that can break and more maintenance than a travel trailer

▷ tricky to pack and unpack

▷ shorter camping season because of greater exposure to the elements

▷ difficult to repeatedly set up and break down on trips with multiple stops

▷ new units are surprisingly expensive

Travel Trailers

Travel trailers are conventional, towable RVs that have hard walls on all four sides. Most of them have bathrooms, kitchens, and various sleeping arrangements that range from basic to luxurious. Our second RV was an affordable Jayco bunkhouse travel trailer, and it served us perfectly for more than six years. An RV with a bunkhouse has a separate dedicated room or closet-like space with bunk beds in it. This was a perfect set up for us, because the boys could go to sleep in their own small room, and we could close the door, stay up, and read in the main living area. This trailer, which weighed about 6,000 pounds, caused us very little trouble, and annual maintenance costs were low. Our Chevy Silverado half-ton pickup was capable of towing over 8,000 pounds, and it did a great job pulling the trailer.

Pros of a Travel Trailer

▷ smaller models may be towable by the family SUV

▷ easy to set up compared to a pop-up camper

▷ ample storage for gear, bedding, and food

▷ if you already own a compatible truck or SUV, travel trailers are affordable compared to motorhomes

▷ wide variety of floor plans and many family-friendly options

▷ no engine maintenance

Cons of a Travel Trailer

▷ may require a large (and possibly expensive) truck to tow, depending on length and weight

▷ can be very large and difficult to store

▷ if you live in a homeowners association, it might not be allowed in your driveway

▷ can be dark and cavelike inside and feel disconnected from nature

Hybrid Travel Trailers

Hybrid travel trailers combine elements of the pop-up camper and the traditional travel trailer. They are hard-walled on all sides, but the front and back
have beds with canvas siding that folds down. We rented a hybrid for a trip
to South Dakota, and we loved it. It was compact and maneuverable when
the bed end was tucked in and fairly spacious when it was fully extended.

Pros of a Hybrid Travel Trailer

▷ lightweight compared to travel
  trailers
▷ shorter length makes for easier
  storage
▷ tent ends allow for an immersive
  experience in nature
▷ easy to pack and lots of storage
▷ ample sleeping options, with
  some floor plans offering three
  full-size beds

Cons of a Hybrid Travel Trailer

▷ canvas maintenance
▷ condensation issues related to the
  canvas
▷ more set up than a travel trailer
▷ more money than a pop-up camper
▷ shorter camping season due to
  exposure to the elements

Fifth Wheels

Fifth wheels are travel trailers with raised forward sections that create a bi-level floor plan. They connect to the bed of a pickup truck using a fifth wheel hitch. We have never camped in a fifth wheel, but we are constantly impressed by their spacious and comfortable floor plans. Many of our friends own "fivers" and love them. They are often referred to as the Cadillacs of the towable RV world.

Pros of a Fifth Wheel

▷ residential design and amenities

▷ private master bedroom for Mom and Dad

▷ ample storage and comfort for long-term travel

▷ easier to tow than a conventional travel trailer

▷ easier to unhitch and set up than a conventional travel trailer

Cons of a Fifth Wheel

▷ most require heavy-duty (expensive!) pickup trucks for towing

▷ often very long and difficult to maneuver and park in tight campgrounds

▷ difficult to achieve good gas mileage while towing

▷ high profile can bang into trees and create problems at low overpasses

Toy Haulers

Toy haulers are RVs that have rear cargo doors that drop down for the loading and unloading of all kinds of gear and equipment, including golf carts, ATVs, motorcycles, bikes, kayaks, and stand-up paddleboards (SUPs). We currently own a toy hauler and love how easily we can pack bikes, kayaks, SUPs, and all of our camp kitchen gear. A toy hauler can be a travel trailer, a fifth wheel, or a motorhome.

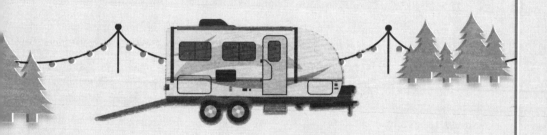

Pros of a Toy Hauler

▷ ample interior space for storing gear and toys
▷ opening the rear door, if you have a screen, provides lovely views and breezes
▷ ample sleeping space for larger families
▷ open and flexible floor plans that can be converted into office spaces, etc.
▷ wide variety of sizes and price points

Cons of a Toy Hauler

▷ taller and wider profile (often up to 102 inches wide) can lower gas mileage
▷ taller and wider profile can be less maneuverable
▷ furniture and interior designs can be more stoic and less residential
▷ often require heavy-duty pickup trucks for safe towing

Class A Motorhomes

Class A motorhomes are constructed and designed on special motor-vehicle chassis with relatively flat front ends and a wide variety of diesel or gas engines. These are self-contained vehicles and do not require a tow vehicle.

Pros of a Class A Motorhome

▷ residential design and appliances

▷ luxurious optional equipment

▷ storage capacity for extended travel

▷ extremely comfortable for extended driving

▷ comfortable floor-plan options for couples without kids

Cons of a Class A Motorhome

▷ significantly higher price points than towable RVs

▷ significantly higher maintenance costs than towable RVs

▷ fewer floor-plan options for families than towable RVs

▷ most Class A owners also tow a car or small SUV to get around

▷ larger Class As can be difficult to maneuver in tight spaces

Class B Motorhomes

Class B motorhomes are van campers that are built using automotive-manufactured van chassis, such as the Mercedes-Benz Sprinter, Ford Transit, or Dodge Ram ProMaster.

Pros of a Class B Motorhome

▷ easy to drive and store

▷ can be used as a daily driver or family vehicle

▷ no tow vehicle required

▷ can fit in almost any campsite

▷ great for couples and solo travelers

▷ maintain their value better than other RVs

Cons of a Class B Motorhome

▷ high price points

▷ significantly less living space than other RVs

▷ significantly less storage space than other RVs

▷ can be difficult to park when exploring urban areas and crowded tourist spots

▷ difficult to find used inventory for sale at dealerships

Class C Motorhomes

Class C motorhomes are built on truck chassis and can often be easily distinguished from Class As because of the bed that overhangs the driving area.

Pros of a Class C Motorhome

- family-friendly floor plans with lots of beds
- automotive truck chassis is relatively easy to maintain and service
- more spacious and comfortable for travel than a pickup truck
- ample storage space and room for food and gear
- drives and maneuvers like a large truck, not a bus
- typically has a lower price point than a Class A

Cons of a Class C Motorhome

- significantly more expensive than most towable RVs
- more maintenance than towable RVs
- you will probably need to tow a smaller vehicle to explore your destination
- low cargo-carrying capacity
- poor gas mileage compared to many truck/trailer combinations

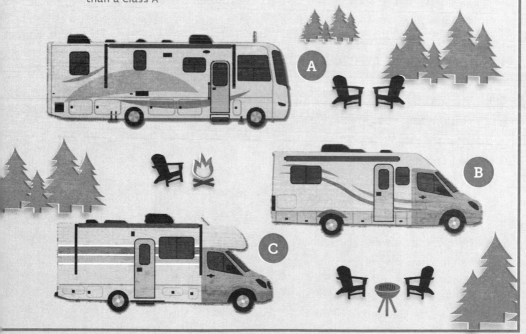

Once you have narrowed down your RV type, it's time to start shopping. But the first thing you need to understand is that shopping for a new RV is very different from shopping for a new car or truck. While there may be some similarities, there are many more differences. Chances are you have dozens of car dealerships, representing every major brand, within a short drive from your house. This is not the case with RV dealerships. They can be spread out far and wide. So while you may have a local RV dealership nearby (we consider a dealer within a two-hour drive to be "local"), you may also need to drive a few hours to a nonlocal dealer to find the RV of your choice, or you may need to buy at an RV show. These are all good options, but there are three important things to consider with each.

Purchasing from a Local Dealer

1 **Purchasing locally is very convenient for shopping.** Shopping at a local dealer saves you precious drive time and, if they have your dream RV, may just be the ideal situation.

2 **Purchasing locally is very convenient for warranty service after the sale.** Every RV needs to go in for either warranty service or basic maintenance at some point. When the dealer is close to home, a trip to the shop can be very convenient—or at least not too inconvenient!

3 **A local dealer may not have your dream RV or preferred brand.** Very few dealers carry every, or even most, RV brands. So, if there is a certain dream RV that tickles your fancy, you may need to expand your search geographically to find it.

Purchasing from a Nonlocal Dealer

1 **Purchasing from a nonlocal dealer can greatly expand your RV brand options.** If your local dealer doesn't carry your favorite brand, don't despair; just get ready to drive farther to find it.

2 **Expanding the reach of your search may also increase your bargaining power.** The more dealers you look at geographically, the more bargaining power you have when it comes to negotiating a purchase price.

3 **Purchasing nonlocally may not be convenient for warranty work or maintenance after the sale.** This might be our most important tip—so listen up! If you do end up buying your dream RV far from home, are you prepared to drive it back to the dealership for warranty work and maintenance? We strongly recommend that you call around to your local dealers to see if they will do warranty service on an RV purchased at another dealership. Having a game plan for this type of situation will save you a lot of irritation in the long run.

Purchasing at an RV Show

RV shows are typically three-to-four-day events where multiple dealers rent out floor space at an arena or conference center to sell their goods. A small RV show may only have a handful of dealers present, while large ones like the Hershey RV Show in Pennsylvania and the Florida RV SuperShow in Tampa might have dozens, if not hundreds, of dealers present. A good RV show will also have vendors selling RV parts and accessories, as well as campground owners advertising their campgrounds and possibly giving out coupons or raffling off free camping nights. I recommend wearing a pair of comfortable shoes and bringing lots of water! You should also take pictures of the prices, names, and floor plans of RVs that interest you, otherwise you will forget everything that you learned! Here are six things to keep in mind before considering purchasing an RV from an RV show:

1 **RV shows have a carnival-like atmosphere, making for a fun shopping experience.** We love going to RV shows because they are a complete hoot! RV owners are a tribe of happy and adventurous folks—when we go to shows, we feel like we are among our people, and you will too.

2 **Free educational seminars prepare you for RV ownership.** Many RV shows have free seminars about maintenance, RV travel, and RV culture. As a potential newbie RV owner, there is so much to learn, and you can learn a whole lot of it by attending a good seminar. Bonus points if Stephanie and I are giving the seminar!

3 **Shows offer many brands and floor plans to explore all in one place.** While a good local dealership may carry three or four brands and dozens of floor plans, a good RV show will give you a chance to look at dozens of brands and hundreds of floor plans. A massive national RV show will enable you to look at the vast majority of RVs in production. Bring good walking shoes!

4 **RV show pricing is very good because many dealers are competing in one place.** If you are not a big fan of heavy negotiating but still want a great price, an RV show may hit the sweet spot for you. RV show prices really do tend to be very competitive—dealers are competing with each other and they are motivated to move a lot of inventory in one day.

5 **You don't get to drive the rig home that day.** You will need to pick up your RV at the dealership, even if you buy it at a show. The dealer will want to prepare the rig for you and give you a walk-through to teach you all of the RV's systems and operating procedures.

6 **You also don't get to inspect the dealer's facility—which is incredibly important!** Buying from a quality dealer is just as important as buying a quality RV. If a dealer has an impressive facility with friendly, well-trained staff and a service department with many bays, those are all signs that they are a great dealer. But you can't inspect any of those things at an RV show, can you?

Hopefully these pros and cons help you make a wise decision when it comes time to buy your first, or next, RV! But the newbie learning curve does not end after you purchase your first RV. Now you have to learn how to use it!

Have you ever watched someone trying to learn a new skill? Think of children learning to ride a bike. At first, they will require a lot of assistance, such as training wheels or a parent running alongside them. Eventually, they'll make some independent strides of their own—with plenty of wobbling and crashing involved. After a while, they'll get it. And they'll soar off down the street on their way to many wonderful adventures.

---------------- **Tips for Buying a Used RV** ----------------

You can get a great deal buying a used RV...but you can also get hosed if you don't know what you're doing. Here are some quick tips if you decide to go this route:

❖ Pay a bit more to buy used from a reputable dealer with a great service center if you are not handy or familiar with RV systems and construction.

❖ If a deal seems too good to be true, it probably is. There are a ton of RV scams on Craigslist, eBay, and Facebook Marketplace, so take appropriate precautions.

❖ Never purchase a used RV without a clean title.

❖ Consider hiring a certified RV inspector to look over a unit. Local inspectors can be found at nrvia.org.

❖ Try to look at a unit right after a good rainstorm, and never purchase a used RV with any signs of water damage.

New RV owners may find themselves facing a similar situation. If it's been a long time since you learned something new, it can be intimidating to suddenly find yourself asking stressful questions like, "How in the world am I going to get this trailer through a tight gas station parking lot?" Or, "Will I be able to empty the black tank without spilling it everywhere?" Or, "Am I hitching up my truck to my trailer properly? Am I going to damage my rig?"

We've been RVing for ten years now, but we still remember the nervousness we faced before our first trip. Even once we became seasoned RVers, we still faced the same apprehension every time we pulled out for a journey with a newer, bigger rig. The good news is that we can assure you that our unease was soon replaced with enthusiasm as we became accustomed to our new equipment.

We firmly believe that even the most intimidated newbie can quickly become comfortable and confident. Are you feeling a little bit nervous and edgy about towing an RV for the first time? That's okay. It really is! We know you will get over those nerves more quickly than you think, especially if you read the following nine tips for gaining confidence as a new RV owner.

Get out your notebook, or just take some notes in the margins. The greatest adventure of your life is just around the corner—and we want to help you get to the fun part faster. Our hard-earned experience is about to take the stage.

The Best RV Shows in America

- The Florida RV SuperShow takes place every January in Tampa, Florida. RVers come from around the country to check out more than 1,500 RVs and enjoy the carnivalesque atmosphere.

- The Hershey RV Show takes place every September and calls itself "America's Largest RV Show"—though the Florida RV SuperShow begs to differ. It is certainly big, hosting more than forty manufacturers. Plus, it's right next door to Hersheypark. So after RV shopping, you can ride the coasters and tour Chocolate World.

- The California RV Show takes place every October in Pomona and is the largest RV shopping opportunity on the West Coast every year. The show has over 1 million square feet of RVs, so bring your walking shoes and plenty of water.

- GS Media & Events is a subsidiary of Good Sam Enterprises that hosts more than twenty-five RV, camping, and boating shows around the country every winter. You can check out www.gsevents.com to look for a show in your neck of the woods.

Nine Tips for Gaining Confidence as a New RV Owner

1 Camp close to home for your first few trips. Now that you've bought the RV of your dreams, it's time to hit those dream destinations, right? Not so fast. For your first few trips, you'll want to book campgrounds close to home. This will allow you to gain confidence as you learn how to operate your new rig. Also, it takes a few trips to figure out what to stock in your RV. If you camp close to home, you can easily run home or to a big-box store to grab the must-have items, and you'll be in familiar territory.

2 Reserve a private campground for your first trip. If you want to spark an internet debate, just ask the people on an RV forum whether public parks or private campgrounds are better. Campgrounds at state and national parks are often more beautiful, but there are some added benefits and amenities that make private campgrounds a better choice for your first trip.

Case in point, they often have full hookups. Until you understand your rig and your family's needs, it's better to have electricity, water, and sewer on-site. Also, private parks often have helpful staff members who can assist with things like backing into a site for the first time.

3 Reserve a pull-through site at your first campground. There are many beautiful campsites in this nation. Some are easy to pull right into, while others require backing in at tight angles while trying to avoid trees and site markers. You will eventually be able to maneuver your trailer

into practically any spot with
ease, but you can avoid some
headaches for your first trip by
booking a pull-through site.
A pull-through site is one that
is situated between two roads,
making it easy to pull right in
when you arrive and pull right
out when you leave...no backing up required. On your first
trip, you have enough to worry
about without having to back
up and angle a trailer into a
spot. Keep it easy-peasy with a
pull-through!

4 **Divide and conquer during
setup.** Arriving at a campground is much different from
checking into a hotel. Quite a
few tasks need to be done in
order to secure your trailer and
set up a cozy campsite. Doing
these for the first time takes a
lot longer than it will eventually
take once you've mastered your
RV. If you have younger kids,
the easiest thing to do is to get
them out from underfoot so
that one adult can truly concen-
trate on setup, while the other
concentrates on keeping the

kids happy and safe. If you have
older kids, they can help with
the setup process.

5 **Don't be afraid to ask for help.**
Not the type of person to ask
for help from random strangers? Get over it. RV owners are
notoriously friendly and helpful
people—and many of them are
at least moderately handy. As
you are learning to operate a
new rig, there will undoubtedly
be some tasks you forget how
to do or never learned in the
first place. Don't be afraid to ask
for help. Most of your neighbors were in your shoes at one
time or another and will kindly
pay it forward.

6 **Don't be afraid to say no to
help when backing in.** One of
the silly things that can stress
newbies out is feeling like other
RVers are judging them while
they're backing in their shiny
new rigs. For reasons unknown
to us, there are some people
who like to kick back in their
camp chairs and watch other
RVers set up camp. Some will

eagerly jump in and offer to "help," which is great—except when it isn't. If you don't want the help, don't worry about politely declining. Simply say, "Hey, we are new at this, and we want to learn how to do it. We'll let you know if we need some assistance!"

7 Expect the unexpected—and don't let it get you down. Things go wrong. It's inevitable. Maybe you'll discover a leak beneath your sink on your first trip, or maybe you'll break something due to "user error." Stuff happens. Try not to lose too much of your vacation time fretting over mistakes and mishaps. Do your best to solve the problem and move on. When you get frustrated, just remember that we have all been in those situations at one time or another.

8 Avoid driving at night. If possible, plan on driving and setting up during daylight hours on your first few trips. Driving at night can be risky. If you break down, you'll have a harder time finding help, since auto-parts stores, garages, and RV dealerships will be closed. Setting up at night in an unfamiliar setting can also be more difficult and nerve-racking.

9 Breathe. Go slow. Have fun. Things will eventually get easier! You will soon be able to set up camp blindfolded. Until then, all you can do is be patient with yourself as you learn. Don't be too self-critical... and don't forget to have fun along the way.

Once you get your first-time jitters out of the way and gain some useful experience of your own, you will relax and settle into the joys of RV ownership. All of the anxiety and trepidation will melt away. The road ahead of you will be filled with serendipitous adventure. You will take your dream RV to your dream destinations. Pretty soon, you'll be like the kid on the bike, pedaling fast with a smile on your face. We know this is true because that's what happened to us. We gained confidence quickly, and all of the anxiety turned into epic family fun.

So, did purchasing a pop-up camper make our family as happy as the family in that Go RVing television commercial that I watched ten years ago?

Yes.

I am almost certain. During those brief stretches of time when our boys stop wrestling and arguing over every godforsaken thing, I'm pretty sure the answer is yes.

W hen we bought our first pop-up camper, we had ridiculously limited knowledge of campgrounds. In fact, we could proba- bly count on one hand the number of campgrounds both of us had visited in our entire lives. But it was May, and there was an RV sitting in our driveway. We were both jumping out of our skin to start using the darn thing. So I did a Google search, found a nearby state park, and booked a site.

It was...rustic, to say the least.

There were no hookups, so we couldn't plug our fancy pop-up camper into electricity or hook the hose up to water and actually use all the bells and whistles we had just splurged on. The ground was a very special com- bination of soil and sand that stuck to our boys like glitter on a glue stick. Plus, the bathhouse had a slick layer of mildew on the floor and colonies of spiders in the rafters. Let's just say I went without a shower that weekend.

We learned quickly that there is a tremendous variety of campgrounds out there, and our family was not particularly suited to scruffy state parks in the Pinelands of New Jersey.

On our very next camping trip, we reserved a site at Seashore Campsites & RV Resort in Cape May, which had a pool, multiple playgrounds, a lake with a beach, and an ice-cream stand. We had found our camping bliss.

Now, there's nothing wrong with rustic, woodsy campgrounds that offer no amenities at all. In fact, some campers live for that sort of weekend escape. But personally, we weren't into roughing it all that much. Our lives as working parents with twin babies were rough enough, thank you very much.

In our first season of camping, we learned that there was as much variety in campgrounds as there is in hotels. While we intuitively knew the difference between a Red Roof Inn and a Four Seasons, we had to learn to find campgrounds that fit both our camping style and our family budget.

You see, there's no such thing as the perfect campground. But there is a perfect campground *for you.* Knowing what you are looking for in terms of both natural beauty and amenities might be the most important part of having amazing camping adventures. Want a peaceful escape without any cell signal or Wi-Fi, where you can gaze up at the stars? You can have that. Want a bustling resort with waterslides, golf carts, restaurants, and outdoor movies? You can find that also.

The most important thing is knowing what you want, and that can be tricky to figure out when you don't have a lot of camping experience. It took a few years of trial and error, but now it's easy for us to spot a campground that will be a good fit for our family. Here's what you need to know to begin building your own campground wish list.

Public and Private Campgrounds

There are two main categories of campgrounds: public and private. Now, there is a lot of variety within these two categories, but there are also some overarching qualities that it helps to be aware of. Some of the following points are certainly generalizations that don't apply to every single campground in each category, but we think they are helpful generalizations that will guide you toward campgrounds your family will love.

Public Campgrounds

Campgrounds that are in county, state, or national parks are considered public campgrounds. Remember that first scrubby campground we stayed at? That was a New Jersey state park campground. The facilities were outdated and the grounds weren't well tended. Other campers were partying late into the night, and there were no rangers on-site to enforce quiet hours. Unfortunately, that place probably scared us away from discovering other wonderful public campgrounds for the duration of our first camping season.

The next year, we spent a couple of nights at Camden Hills State Park in midcoast Maine and discovered how amazing a state park camping experience could be. We had an enormous site with plenty of room for the boys to play. We were just steps from some great hikes within the park. I'll never forget the clean bathhouses with lots of hot water and amazing water pressure. Oh, and we paid about a third of what the private KOA camping site cost us at our next stop in Maine.

Pros of Public Campgrounds

⇝ Public campgrounds are significantly cheaper than private campgrounds, sometimes costing a third or even half of the price—think $20 to $30 per night as opposed to $50 and up.

⇝ Public campgrounds almost always have larger, more private sites.

⇝ Public campgrounds are often in the most beautiful locations in each region. Think oceanfront sites or mountaintop views.

⇝ Public campgrounds often offer on-site activities, such as nature programs, hiking, biking, and fishing.

Cons of Public Campgrounds

⇝ Public campgrounds often lack water, electric, and sewer hookups at individual sites. There is a huge range of quality in the shared bathrooms and showers.

⇝ Reservations can be very difficult to make at the most popular public campgrounds. You usually need to book online or call a contracted company that handles reservations. These companies have limited knowledge about individual campgrounds.

⇝ Campgrounds are often booked up to a year in advance. People covet these beautiful and affordable campsites. This is inconvenient for folks who don't know their vacation schedule that far out.

⇝ Because of the lower price, some public campgrounds attract large groups who want to stay up late and party.

It used to be assumed that a public campground wouldn't offer amenities like electric and sewer hookups for RVs. That has changed quite a bit over the last decade. While most national parks still lack these amenities (and are sometimes referred to as "dry" campgrounds), many states have upgraded their campground facilities in an attempt to attract tourist dollars. States like Florida, South Carolina, Missouri, Arkansas, and Oregon have reputations for beautiful campgrounds with water and electric hookups and modern amenities. One of the most famous public campgrounds in the country is in James Island County Park near Charleston, South Carolina. There you'll find electric hookups, miles of hiking and biking trails, a splash park, and a climbing wall.

Some campers only ever stay at public campgrounds. They love the natural beauty combined with the cheap price tag. Navigating the reservation system can be the biggest hurdle to camping at some of the most popular public campgrounds in the country. What you really have to do is get in the spirit of competitive online booking. Just try to imagine that you are buying Taylor Swift tickets for your preteen and you should be fine.

-------------- **Our Top Six Public Campgrounds** --------------

1. Blue Bell Campground at Custer State Park, South Dakota
2. Assateague State Park, Maryland
3. Schoodic Woods Campground, Acadia National Park, Maine
4. James Island County Park, South Carolina
5. Graves Island Provincial Park, Nova Scotia, Canada
6. Fort De Soto Park Campground, Florida

Private Campgrounds

The world of private campgrounds is even more varied than that of public campgrounds. Some are small, independent mom-and-pop operations.

Others are franchises or owned by large corporations. We've stayed in RV parks that were practically parking lots by the side of a busy highway, and we've stayed in RV resorts that would rival an all-inclusive hotel on a Caribbean island.

To be honest, private campgrounds were particularly appealing to us when we were newbie campers with little tykes in tow. Reservations were easy to make, and there was always someone there to help us back into our campsite. When our boys were little, it was a godsend to have a playground and a pool. And grabbing some milk at the camp store instead of having to track down a grocery store saved us more than once.

Pros of Private Campgrounds

→» Private campgrounds almost always offer full hookups at each site. You'll have no worries about messy public bathhouses and midnight potty runs.

→» Most private campgrounds offer extensive amenities. Think pools, playgrounds, game rooms, miniature golf, and basketball courts.

→» It is almost always easier to book reservations at a private campground. You can pick up the phone and talk to someone from the campground. They can answer specific questions and recommend sites.

Cons of Private Campgrounds

→» Private campgrounds are more expensive. You get more in the way of amenities and hookups, but you pay more too. Generally, private campgrounds cost $50 to $100 per night, depending on the season and location.

⇥ Sites are almost always smaller and less private at private campgrounds. Campground owners are in business to maximize profits, which can often mean minimizing the size of individual sites.

⇥ Tiny temptations abound. Private campgrounds sell soda, candy, ice cream, and cheap toys. Depending on the age and inclinations of your kids, as well as how "commercial" the campground is, you may feel like you are camping at a boardwalk or amusement park.

CAMPGROUND FRANCHISES

Knowing about the larger campground franchises may help you navigate the world of private campgrounds and not get too overwhelmed. Kampgrounds of America (KOA) has more than five hundred franchised campgrounds in the United States and Canada. The amenities and activities offered at all these campgrounds vary widely. However, KOA fans love that they can expect a certain level of customer service and security no matter where they are. A "yellow shirt" (what they call their staff) will escort you to your site and help you back in. They'll deliver firewood and ice right to your camper. And there is always a dog park where your furry family member can run free.

Membership Clubs

Looking to get the most bang for your camping buck? Here are some membership clubs that may or may not be good for you, depending on how and where you like to camp:

- Good Sam Club
- KOA Value Kard Rewards
- Thousand Trails
- Passport America
- Club Yogi Rewards

KOA has particularly invested in its tenting sites and cabin rentals over the last few years. Tent campers will often find electric hookups, raised tent platforms, and cooking shelters. The premium cabins available for rent have towels and bedding, plus fully stocked kitchens. We've stayed in dozens of KOAs over the last decade. While they might not always be the largest, most beautiful sites, we feel safe and the kids have a blast. A well-reviewed KOA is a great place to try your hand at family camping.

Yogi Bear's Jellystone Park Camp-Resorts is another franchise to put in your campground-booking wheelhouse. These campgrounds are independently owned and pay a licensing fee to use the Yogi Bear's Jellystone branding. We visited our first Jellystone when the boys were five years old, and we've been to dozens more since then. It really wouldn't be a complete season of camping for our family without a visit to see Yogi Bear and his friends.

There are more than eighty Jellystone campgrounds in North America. The experience does vary quite a bit, depending on which one you visit, so you have to do your research to find the resort-style Jellystones that our family loves so very much. The campgrounds in Kerrville, Texas; Quarryville, Pennsylvania; and Williamsport, Maryland have huge water-slides, zip lines, go-cart courses, and laser-tag tournaments. Our visits to Jellystones are definitely more about crazy family fun than peace and relaxation, but the kids' enjoyment makes up for our adult exhaustion at the end of the vacation.

RESORT CAMPGROUNDS

One of the biggest trends in the camping industry is the rise of resort camp-grounds. Ten years ago, there were a handful of these scattered around the country, such as Normandy Farms in Foxborough, Massachusetts, and Cherry Hill Park in College Park, Maryland. Now it seems like new multimillion-dollar campground resorts are opening every year.

Our Top Six Resort Campgrounds

1. Disney's Fort Wilderness Resort and Campground, Florida

2. Yogi Bear's Jellystone Park, Quarryville, Pennsylvania

3. Massey's Landing, Delaware

4. Sandy Pines Campground, Kennebunkport, Maine

5. Normandy Farms, Foxborough, Massachusetts

6. Rafter J Bar Ranch, Hill City, South Dakota

This trend has been hugely popular with families. Some campers complain about the prices, but these resorts are selling out up to a year in advance. Clearly, people are willing to pay for the luxuries provided.

What is the difference between a regular ole campground and a resort campground? It's a combination of both the amenities and activities provided on-site. The best ones create an environment where you don't want or need to leave at any time during your stay. They have indoor and outdoor pools, spas, water parks, mini-golf courses, jumping pillows, and arcades. They'll have a complete schedule of activities so your kids can be entertained at every hour of the day. Some also have a slate of adult-centered activities like yoga, water aerobics, and watercolor classes.

Now, some cranky people on the interwebs like to repeatedly argue that this sort of vacation is *not camping*. The world has definitely moved on from the idea that camping is mostly about taking a tent into the woods and disconnecting from civilization for a few days. The good news is that this kind of experience still exists if you want it. We have camped in a Badlands National Park campground and a Sioux Falls Jellystone within the same week. For us, campground variety is truly the spice of our travel life. There's a campground for everyone right now, you just have to know how to find it.

Making Your Campground Wish List

In our first few months of camping, we stayed at a state park, a private family campground, and a KOA resort on the beach in Cape Hatteras. It didn't take us long to figure out what we really loved in a campground. You'll want to develop your own wish list for a perfect campground...and remember that it might change over the years.

When our boys were little, a playground and a pool made all the difference in the world. Now they would rather have a basketball court and organized sports activities. We also travel with our dog now, which means we almost always need electric hookups to keep her cool on hot days. I used to hate to be at waterfront sites when the boys weren't independent swimmers yet. Now a waterfront site is just about heaven in a handbasket.

> ----- **Top Five Considerations in Selecting a Campground** -----
> 1. Clean and well-maintained bathhouse/restrooms
> 2. "Kid friendly"
> 3. Self-guided recreational activities
> 4. Allows pets and has a pet area
> 5. Free Wi-Fi
>
> *(KOA, 2018 North American Camping Report)*

If you haven't done a lot of camping in the past, answering the following five questions will help you develop a campground wish list for your family:

1 **What's my ideal campground location?** With many camping destinations, you'll have a choice between staying at a busy campground close to regional attractions and staying at a quieter spot a bit farther away.

You have to decide if you are willing to sacrifice space and scenery to be right in the middle of the action.

Our Top Six Campgrounds Near Urban Destinations

1. Indiana Dunes State Park, near Chicago
2. Cherry Hill Park, near Washington, DC
3. Liberty Harbor RV Park, near New York City
4. Philadelphia South/Clarksboro KOA, near Philadelphia
5. San Francisco RV Resort, near San Francisco
6. French Quarter RV Resort, New Orleans

Some folks love feeling a million miles away from everything when they camp. Before booking, realize that this might mean long drives to the grocery store, as well as spotty internet and cell-phone connectivity. On the other hand, travelers who want to be near the most popular area attractions might have to deal with some road noise. Decide what suits you best and then narrow down your options from there.

Which amenities are necessary, and which ones are optional? Campgrounds vary tremendously in the level of amenities available, so make sure to choose one that checks the right boxes on your personal wish list. Do you love to end every day swimming in the pool or relaxing in the hot tub? Or are you looking for a campground with direct access to hiking trails and bike paths? Maybe you just want a simple, no-frills base camp for exploring the nearby area.

Make sure to decide what you want before diving into online reviews. If you never wash your clothes at the campground, ignore comments on the condition of the laundry facilities. Likewise, if you use the bathroom in your RV, immaculate comfort stations shouldn't be on your list of priorities. Other amenities to consider include playgrounds, Wi-Fi access, bike and boat rentals, organized activities, and fitness facilities.

③ What type of site is best for my family? Once you have narrowed down your campground options, make sure that they offer the ideal campsite for your family. Are the tent sites level and spacious? Are the RV sites back-ins or pull-throughs, and do they fit your rig? Check on the varying types of RV hookups, including electric, water, and sewer. Are the cabins fully stocked with bedding and linens? I personally hate making cabin beds, so this can be a big deal breaker for me.

Double and triple check that the campsite has the hookups you are seeking. If you are accustomed to running the dishwasher in your motorhome, not having a sewer hookup might be a problem. If you are traveling in a tent trailer during the summer months, you'll probably want electricity at your site to run the air-conditioning.

④ What campsite features do I prefer? Many campgrounds offer a variety of campsite options for their guests. Of course, the typical site includes a picnic table and fire ring, but it has become very popular to offer campsite upgrades. Premium sites may have concrete pads, stone patios, outdoor furniture, decks, and gas grills. Also consider whether you prefer shade or sun and if you would like a waterfront spot, if available.

⑤ Where do I want my spot to be located in the campground? Choosing the right campsite location is almost as important as choosing the right campground. Studying a campground map and speaking with a reservation specialist will help you ensure that you park your rig in a spot that measures up to your expectations.

If you have young kids, being near the playground and pool might be a bonus. If you're traveling without little campers, however, you probably want to be far from all that noise and activity. Also take into consideration the placement of bathhouses, campground entrances, dumpsters, and nearby highways. If you are concerned about connectivity, ask about internet speeds at varying places in the campground.

Online reservations are a modern convenience that many campers enjoy tremendously. However, our experience shows that picking up the phone and chatting with a campground reservationist will often ensure that you are matched with the ideal campsite for your rig and personal preferences. Don't stop at choosing the perfect campground— make sure to get that perfect campsite as well.

Favorite Resources for Campground Reviews

- *Good Sam Guide Series*
- KOA Camping app and directory
- *Campground of the Week* podcast
- *The RV Atlas* podcast
- Allstays app
- RV Parky app
- Campendium website
- TripAdvisor
- CampgroundReviews.com
- The RV Atlas Group (on Facebook)

THE BEACH

FORT WILDERNESS

THE LAKE

GREAT SMOKY MOUNTAINS

It is estimated that ten million Americans suffer from seasonal affective disorder (a.k.a. SAD) and that many millions more suffer from a milder version known as the winter blues. Stephanie and I think that RV owners suffer from a very particular strain of this phenomenon that we like to call the "winterization blues." It can happen anytime after camping season has ended and the RV has been winterized and put into storage until spring.

I usually come down with a severe case of the winterization blues a few weeks after the holiday season has ended. When I walk by the RV in the driveway, I imagine that it is whispering to me, telling me to uncover it and step inside. When this happens, I place my hand on the RV and whisper back, "Soon, my friend, very soon." It's not as weird as it sounds.

Well...okay. Yes it is.

Winter days can be tough, but winter nights are tougher. During the coldest nights of January and February, I often get moody and grim about the month. No Netflix series can capture my attention for more than an episode or two, and no novel can keep me from pacing back and forth in my garage looking for camping gear to clean or repair. How many times can I check that my lanterns and flashlights are fully functional before I need to seek professional help? According to Stephanie, not too many...

We do, on occasion, take to the campground during the winter months, but there are very few places near us that are open after October 31, and sometimes even those have roads that are impassable because of snow and ice. We also fly to Florida every January and rent an RV for a week of camping—but these are only temporary salves for the winterization blues.

So how do I cope when I can't camp? I plan really awesome trips, that's how.

Trip planning, much like camping itself, is therapeutic. If camping is a strong antidote to the woes of the digital age (too much email, too much social media, too much partisan political bickering, too many dumb cat videos), then thoughtful trip planning is a strong antidote to those bleak winter months when so many of us can't camp. Pulling out my camping catalogs and making reservations gives me something to look forward to when the cold pounds against our windows and the summer seems far away.

Our planning philosophy straddles a fruitful middle ground between stringency and serendipity. We are stringent about booking our campgrounds early and not planning many last-second trips. But *our number one travel tip of all time* is to talk to locals while you're on your actual trip and trust their recommendations. That means leaving space open during our vacations for serendipitous discoveries.

Our current operating method is to plan a trip with an understanding of what that location is known for *and* a list of possible activities that we might enjoy. We also have a loose schedule in our minds, since we have discovered that it is easy to miss out on great experiences as a result of not having a grasp on operating hours or tour times. Our actual itinerary on most trips ends up being a combination of planning and kismet. Finding the sweet spot between these two things is always a work in progress.

We also make sure to leave open gaps of time for just hanging out and relaxing at the campground. A long, lazy afternoon of swimming at the campground pool, coupled with grilling at our campsite and relaxing around a campfire after dinner, can easily become one of the best parts of a trip. We recommend that you take time to relax, even if you are staying somewhere epic like Yellowstone, Glacier, or Mount Rushmore. Our everyday lives are often so hectic and fast-paced, and that mentality can creep into a camping vacation as well.

When we slow down on a camping vacation, something magical happens—we get to spend time together with the ones we love the most in beautiful settings. Time spent together in nature strengthens family bonds and introduces us to our best selves. When our children are staring at mountains instead of screens, we see them not as tiny tyrants, but as kindred spirits—and when our partners are hiking beside us, instead of doing laundry beside us, we see them not as burned-out co-parents, but as copilots on a great adventure. And all of this magic starts with trip planning.

Making campground reservations months in advance is also becoming more of a necessity, since RV ownership and interest in camping has exploded and reached a critical mass in American culture. Older RV owners and tent campers often wax poetic about the days when you could hop into your RV or station wagon and take off into the sunset without reservations. This kind of serendipitous travel is still possible, but it has become harder to pull off—particularly if you want the best sites at the best campgrounds.

My obsession with planning camping trips months in advance can drive Stephanie crazy. But once we get on the same page, we are a well-oiled machine. Picking destinations, selecting campgrounds, and even researching local road-food spots is a pleasurable way to spend time together. We even get the kids involved and show them YouTube videos of the places we are researching. Last winter, we showed them short videos about Mount Rushmore and Crazy Horse Memorial that piqued their interest and got them excited for our upcoming adventures.

We strongly recommend that you start your own trip planning as early as possible. It might seem crazy to start a full year ahead of schedule, but it may be necessary if you want to camp at popular spots like Great Smoky Mountains National Park or Walt Disney World's Fort Wilderness. The best campgrounds might not be completely booked a year in advance, but the best individual sites at those campgrounds probably will be.

- - - - - - - **Favorite North American Camping Destinations** - - - - - - -

1. Mountains

2. Forests

3. Lakes and ponds

4. Rivers

5. Oceans

(KOA, 2018 North American Camping Report)

Many RV owners take the same vacations every year and book next summer's site during their current stay. I do this every year at Fort Wilderness, where you can actually make reservations 499 days in advance. If you want to book a camping trip to Disney over the Christmas holiday, or to Great Smoky Mountains National Park over the Fourth of July, you'd better jump to it early!

Of course, Disney and the Smokies are extreme examples, and every location and campground is different. But as a general rule of thumb, start your trip planning six to twelve months in advance for popular destinations. If you call a campground and find that it is totally booked up during your desired stay, you might consider calling back once a week and checking for cancellations. Sometimes I get a little crazy and call back every single day. I've never failed to book a site when I take this aggressive approach. Don't lose hope for taking those spontaneous, last-second trips either. They are still possible, just not guaranteed.

Now that I've convinced you to book your trips early, what are the next steps for planning a great camping adventure? Ask the following three questions to pinpoint your camping bliss.

How Far Are You Willing to Drive?

It's such a simple—but important—question. Many family camping trips go off the rails right away because Mom or Dad wants to drive too far. We learned very quickly that our kids behave like little gentlemen for the first seven hours of a trip but start to act like feral cats soon after. Feral cats stuck in a cage together. Things get ugly fast, especially if we run out of snacks. They start getting in each other's faces and randomly touching each other. God forbid someone should actually fall asleep, because that's when the real torture begins. We have often pushed trips past our seven-hour time limit and regretted it.

When driving to somewhere really far away, like Sleeping Bear Dunes in Michigan or Nova Scotia in the Canadian Maritimes, we often plan one-night stopovers to rest up and recharge our batteries. To save money, we occasionally spend the night at Walmart, Cabela's, Cracker Barrel, or other spots that allow free overnight parking. Please remember to call ahead if you plan on doing this, as local ordinances may not allow it. If you stay at a campground to break up two days of driving, we recommend reserving a pull-through site that is long enough that you don't have to unhitch—this will save time pulling in at night and pulling out in the morning.

Thus far, only our trip to Mount Rushmore has required three full days of driving in a row. It was an epic trip that we will always remember, but by the time we pulled into the driveway at home, Stephanie and I were almost ready to be institutionalized. Each family is different—but I recommend that you find your family's driving limits and try to respect them.

What Type of Camping Vacation Do You Really Want?

When we bought our first RV, we knew we wanted to do lots of beach camping, so we hitched up our pop-up camper and headed to Cape Hatteras for a week of sun, surf, and sand. During the next few summers, we opted for the mountains and headed to Acadia National Park and Great Smoky Mountains National Park. In recent years, I have been dreaming about taking thematic camping trips. I would like to take our boys on a baseball-themed trip that would include stops near major- and minor-league parks and the National Baseball Hall of Fame in Cooperstown, New York. We would end the trip in Cape Cod eating chowder while watching a game in their famous wooden-bat-only collegiate summer baseball league. We have friends who have planned themed camping trips along the Kentucky Bourbon Trail and friends who have planned RV trips to Civil War battlefields.

Urban destinations are also an option. Few major cities have campgrounds in their downtown areas, but many of them do have campgrounds nearby. When we first got into RVing, we were pleasantly surprised to discover that we could set up camp near Boston, New York City, Philadelphia, Charleston, San Antonio, San Francisco, and pretty much any other urban destination, if we were willing to drive into the city or use public transportation near the campground in lieu of staying downtown in a hotel room. We bring our RV to Cherry Hill Park just outside of Washington, DC, every year and pick up public transportation from right inside the campground. Never assume that certain destinations are not friendly for camping trips. More often than not, they are, especially if you are a flexible traveler.

Do You Want a Relaxing Vacation or a High-Octane Adventure?

If you prefer a relaxing camping trip, you might not want to head to Fort Wilderness during Halloween or Christmas. If you want a high-octane camping adventure, you might not want to head to a sleepy beach town during a shoulder season. For us, a relaxing trip almost always means camping on or near the beach. High adventure often means hiking in a gorgeous national park like Olympic in Washington State.

We all define relaxation and adventure differently, and it's important to figure out which you want during any given vacation. The end of the school year is often frantic and stressful for us, so we like to plan a mellow beach vacation over the Fourth of July. We plan our more adventurous trips later in the summer as a last hurrah before school starts. This works well for us, and we encourage you to find what works best for you. If you plan appropriately, relaxation and adventure are possible during the same trip. Believe it or not, this is how we plan our Disney trips. We go crazy in the parks in the morning and early afternoon, then we head back to the campground and relax by the pool before dinner.

Once you have settled on a location and a campground, it's time to start planning out activities for your trip. We recommend creating a list of possibilities and learning which activities require advance reservations and which can be done spontaneously. Here are six tried-and-true tips that have helped us plan our camping adventures over the last decade.

Tip #1: Research the Standard Tourist Activities

The very first thing we do is find out what *everyone* does when they go to a place. Some people avoid all things touristy, but if you visit Yellowstone National Park and don't see Old Faithful, I think you are pretty foolish.

Niagara Falls, the Gateway Arch, and the Golden Gate Bridge are all pretty clichéd tourist attractions that I think everyone should visit. Google, TripAdvisor, Fodor's, Lonely Planet, and U.S. News & World Report Travel will all give you great results for "Top Ten Things to Do" searches. You can read the reviews, compare lists, pick a couple of must-sees, and move on.

---------- **Digital Resources for Trip Planning** -----------

⟡ *The RV Atlas* podcast

⟡ The RV Atlas Group (on Facebook)

⟡ Roadtrippers

⟡ TripAdvisor

⟡ Google reviews

⟡ Roadside America

Tip #2: Let Yourself Get a Little Weird

Apps like Roadtrippers and Roadside America will guide you to offbeat sites that may not be in the traditional travel guides. I *always* cross-check any of these recommendations with other review sites to gauge people's enjoyment of the attraction. Because weird is sometimes better...but not always.

Tip #3: Search for Area Festivals

Check out any festivals that will be happening during the dates you are visiting a destination. I will never forget the blueberry festival that we stumbled upon in Vermont or the "farm frolic" that we found in rural Pennsylvania. There are apps and websites where you can search for these things, but I personally like to visit the Convention and Visitors Bureau (CVB) website before I arrive. Or—*gasp*—call them! These people know everything about what is happening in their towns. Use the local expertise.

Tip #4: Know Your Family's Favorites

Apart from the above research, I also do searches for types of activities and attractions that have proven to be big hits with our boys every time. I always look for local nature centers, which often aren't listed in tourist guides. Other crowd-pleasing standards? Botanical gardens, children's gardens, boat tours, kayak tours, animal sanctuaries, nature preserves, children's museums, science centers, minor-league baseball stadiums, and popular local park spaces. I search for all of these independently and am amazed by what I discover that is not included in popular travel resources. The generic travel guides for any given destination will only take you so far. Dig deeper, camper. Dig deeper.

Tip #5: Know the Culinary Highlights

For us, food is an integral part of our traveling experience and one of our favorite ways to enjoy local culture. We always consult the book *Roadfood*, by Jane and Michael Stern, before every trip to find out if there are any must-visit roadside joints along our route. If there is a local specialty or delicacy (think "Michigan" hot dogs in New York State and lobster rolls in Cape Cod), we plan ahead of time to track down the best of the best.

Print Resources

- ✦ *Good Sam Travel Guide Series*
- ✦ *Idiots' Guides: RV Vacations*
- ✦ *Roadfood*
- ✦ Moon Travel Guides
- ✦ Appalachian Mountain Club (AMC) guides
- ✦ Wildsam Field Guides

Tip #6: Let Great Books Inspire You

We are so entrenched in internet and app culture that sometimes we forget about literature and travel writing and *actual books*. Find out if there are any great books written about your destination or stories that take place there. Reading *The Lobster Coast* and *The Lobster Chronicles* before visiting coastal Maine will give you an entirely different understanding of the region, as well as dozens of ideas for day trips and local activities. For the fiction fan, reading a novel like *The Prince of Tides* by Pat Conroy will enrich any Low Country adventure. Driving cross-country? We hope you get your hands on a copy of *Travels with Charley: In Search of America* by John Steinbeck.

Putting relevant books in the hands of your children before a camping vacation will also increase their curiosity about the region you are visiting. Before we visited Washington State, we bought *I Survived the Eruption of Mount St. Helens, 1980* by Lauren Tarshis. Both of our older sons devoured it and were particularly excited about that stop on our Pacific Northwest road trip.

◻

When you fall head over heels in love with camping, there can be a few negative side effects. For instance, you might find yourself unhappy at home with a severe case of the winterization blues. While Stephanie and I are big believers in living our best lives at home and at the campground, we both realize that the winter can get long and hard. We combat the cold by dreaming of summer hikes and waterfront campsites—and then we do the legwork that will eventually make those dreams a reality. We hope you take your trip planning seriously, but leave room for serendipitous discoveries and profound relaxation.

We hope that you find your bliss at the campground. Just remember that the journey often starts at home on those long, dreary winter nights. So turn off the TV and stop scrolling through your newsfeed on Facebook. Pull out a few maps, some camping catalogs, and maybe even a travel journal filled with blank pages.

Look at each word that you write down as a footstep that will lead you toward a great adventure.

CHAPTER

Seven

The Art of

PACKING AND
UNPACKING

STEPHANIE

ur first camping trips taught us two very valuable lessons:

1. Camping with our kids was bringing adventure and fun back into our family life.

2. Packing and unpacking from these trips was far from a joyful experience and usually ended with hollering, the silent treatment, or a combination of both.

Anyone with kids knows how hard it can be just to get out of the house. Going to the neighborhood grocery store is a challenge, much less heading to the campground for the weekend. Some parents cry uncle early on and simply give up. We get that. We were beach-loving parents who barely saw the ocean for a couple of years because it was just too hard. The work wasn't worth the reward.

On the other hand, the rewards of our family camping trips were turning out to be pretty stinking great very early on. We had discovered a way to have quality family time that was also fun. We were spending more time outside than ever before, and Jeremy and I were connecting as a couple again. We were emerging out of that new parent haze and seeing a world of possibility stretched out before us. Finding fun campgrounds, making trip plans with friends, sitting around the campfire with a glass of wine at night... We were completely and totally invigorated by this new world of adventure.

But in the spirit of complete and total transparency, we were failing pretty hard at the packing and unpacking part of this new hobby. First of all, it seemed to take us forever. We would set a time for departure, but hours later, we'd still be scurrying back and forth from the house to the RV carrying God knows what. Second of all, we had no system. We were completely reinventing the wheel with every RV trip. This meant that our weary brains were working overtime, trying to remember *all the stuff* and how we had jigsawed it into the pop-up camper and SUV last time.

Eventually, we realized that if we wanted to keep having these fun camping adventures, we had better get our packing dialed in. There was just no reason for all the pre-trip stress and tension.

Well, we did it. We got our acts together, we created a system, and now we can get out of the house and to the campground without a lot of fuss or bother. In fact, I noted that it took us about thirty minutes to pack for our last cabin-camping trip, and I don't think we forgot a single thing. Not even the doggie doo-doo bags. I clearly patted myself on the back for that one.

Getting Started: Basic Packing Tips

Want to pack with the ease and beauty of a synchronized swim team? Here are the lessons we learned on our journey from being packing zeros to becoming packing heroes.

Have Dedicated Camping Gear

After we bought the pop-up camper, we really didn't want to invest in any new camping gear. It was probably a good financial decision at the time, but that choice also led to a lot of extra work every time we packed. I would have to load up towels, pillows, sheets, and even our kitchen coffee maker every time we went camping. It was totally absurd.

Fast-forward years later, and we have an RV that is 100 percent stocked with everything we need except for food and clothes. It didn't happen overnight, but we slowly added the most important things to our camping-gear collection. We would get a new blender or coffee maker for the house and carry the old one right out to the camper. I got a set of towels when they went on sale at a local department store. We went to IKEA and bought RV pillows for everyone on the cheap. (Speaking of which, if you are on a budget, IKEA is your RV-stocking friend. It's practically a discount camping-supply store in disguise.)

This advice applies to tent and cabin camping as well. We have fully stocked bins in the garage that hold the percolator, fire starters, can opener, and every other little thing that you don't want to worry about when you pack to go camping. It's been a true game changer for our family.

Decide What Type of Camping Trip You Are Packing For

Not every camping trip is the same, yet for some reason, we used to pack like they were. In other words, *all the things* came, whether we were likely to use them or not. Now we are a little smarter about loading up the bikes, kayaks, or paddleboards. If we are going to cabin camp outside of Washington, DC, and enjoy tons of sightseeing, we'll leave the camping "toys" at home. On the flip side, if we're heading out for a two-week summer adventure, it's a total free-for-all, and we want to bring everything we might possibly use.

The same goes for food. In the past, we would act like someone was scoring our campground menu according to a Boy Scout grading scale. The reality is that on some trips, we eat more meals out than we do at the campground, and on others we just keep it super simple and subsist on cereal, PB&J, and a weenie roast. Sometimes we are in the mood to plan and shop for special campfire meals. Other times, we know it's a quick, easy trip that's not going to involve a lot of cooking. Knowing what type of camping trip we are planning for completely focuses our packing energy.

Divide and Conquer

Here's a simple truth in our family: if everyone is in charge of everything, no one is in charge of anything. That's probably the case around your house too. We used to race around the house, bumping into each other, getting in each other's way, and asking, "Did you pack the thingamajig?" a hundred million times. Then there was the fine art of casting blame when said thingamajig was, predictably, left at home.

In fact, it might have been one of those moments that forced us to finally get our packing act together. We arrived at our beautiful beach campground on a Friday afternoon, ready to enjoy a fun and relaxing week-end together. Except that, when I went to change into my bathing suit, I discovered that *all* of my clothing had been left behind. Of course, I blamed Jeremy 100 percent. I had packed everyone's clothes and put them in the front hall for him to move into the camper. But apparently he hadn't known that it was his job to put all those things in the camper. It was a communication breakdown, to say the least.

A quick trip to Ross saved the weekend, and making a clear list of packing jobs for each one of us saved our relationship. We divided our duties according to household location. Anything in the house (clothing, food, linens, medicine, etc.) is my job. Anything outside the house (bikes, coolers, sports equipment, etc.) is his job. This has worked perfectly for us, since we are in our separate spaces and therefore more likely to stay in love while preparing for a trip.

Teach the Kids to Help from Day One (or Close to Day One)

We've been camping since our twin boys were eleven months old, and obviously they weren't much of a help at that point. However, by the time they were two years old, we were already giving them packing tasks that were appropriate for their age. We would have them bring their lovies out to the RV bed, pick out a couple of books, and put their sippy cups and snacks in the car. Over the years, we slowly added more and more responsibilities.

It wasn't easy at first. Like most kids, they would sometimes completely ignore the task at hand or do a very mediocre job. But we stuck with it, and in a few years, they became pretty great packing buddies. The reason we are now able to pack for a cabin-camping trip in about thirty minutes is because our boys take care of their own clothes and gear by themselves. I hand each of them their color-coded set of three packing cubes and tell them how many days we will be traveling. They know the formula: number of days of camping plus one. So, if we're camping for three days, we'll need four pairs of socks, four pairs of undies, four pants, four shirts, etc. When we first started having them pack, I was careful to check that we weren't heading to the campground with a bunch of shorts and tank tops in October. You know, trust but verify. But by the time they were seven years old, they had it pretty much dialed in.

Unpack Right Away, Every Time, without Exception

Look, we are not lazy people. But after a camping trip with the family, it's easy to get flaky about unpacking. You know how people joke about the suitcase that doesn't get unpacked for weeks after a vacation? Well that happens with camping trips too. In our early days, we would roll into the driveway and stumble out of the car, happy but exhausted from our adventures.

I would get the kids in the house and immediately get distracted sorting through the mail or worrying about what was for dinner.

It was a little too easy to ignore the basket of dirty clothes and towels in the RV and the leftover food in the pantry. Monday morning would come around and someone would be searching high and low for their raincoat (it's in the camper!) or their sneakers (they're in the camper!). Over the course of the next week, we would slowly unpack in a haphazard and unorganized way. Then this disorganization would snowball and cause us trouble packing for the next trip.

Now when we return from a trip, we practice something we lovingly refer to as SWAT Team Sunday. (Not that we always return from trips on Sundays, but the nickname came about after our weekend trips and just kind of stuck.) We tell our kids that you have to pay to play, and nobody is off the hook until everything is unpacked and cleaned up. It's actually shocking how quickly this happens when we all work together and no one gets sidetracked by snack time or the backyard trampoline. Dirty laundry goes straight down to the washing machine. Clean laundry goes back into drawers. Food gets put away in the refrigerator and pantry. I'm the general giving orders in the house, and Jeremy's the general outside in the RV. Most of the time, we're completely unpacked within half an hour.

The Balancing Act

When we're road-tripping with our RV or just the family car, it's both a blessing and a curse that we can pack way more than when we're flying on a plane. We've done our fair share of overpacking and underpacking, but we like to think that we've found something of a balance over the years. Of course, as our kids grow, we're constantly changing and adjusting our family routines. Here are seven lessons we've learned along the way:

1 **When traveling with babies and toddlers, being overprepared is way preferable to being underprepared.** When we were camping with eleven-month-old twins, and later with a six-week-old baby, we got ourselves into some pickles. We were minimalists by nature when it came to baby gear, and neither of us was any good about packing a diaper bag, much less a weekend baby bag. I soon realized that I needed a pared-down version of our home setup, including extra wipes, baby blankets, and a truckload of outfit changes. As our boys have gotten older, we've been able to scale back considerably.

2 **Balance familiar items with special items.** As I mentioned before, packing became so much easier once we had all our dedicated camping gear organized and ready to go at any time. That meant some books, games, and toys were permanently housed in the RV and became special treats, only enjoyed while we were on a family camping trip. This worked out even better than we expected, and it was like our kids were getting "new" toys every time we camped. They also started to connect certain games like checkers, Spot It!, and Uno with camping and looked forward to playing them on every trip. The same went with food. I saved certain meals like pie-iron pizzas, slow-cooker

oatmeal, and weenie roasts for camping, and they would look forward to those special treats.

Now, as much as we love to have the camper fully stocked and ready to go, our boys always seem to want the comforts of home on the road. To this day, they carry out their favorite blanket, pillow, or stuffed animal. They also sometimes insist on bringing along their favorite toy of the moment or a stack of new baseball cards. In the food category, our one picky eater can struggle with all the different "camping" meals that get trotted out over a family trip. It really helps him if I bring along some of the foods on his "list" (I know, I know...his words, not mine!) like yogurt, Cheerios, and pizza bagels.

So I guess in a nutshell, our lesson would be to make it special...but not too special.

3   **Don't overdo it on the toys.** If you have the extra space, it can be tempting to bring along a miniature version of the playroom at home. Believe me, we've fallen into that trap and ended up with bins of superheroes spread out across a campsite in the White Mountains of New Hampshire. Although it's certainly nice for kids to have some well-loved toys that will occupy them while you (heaven forbid!) relax in a camp chair for five minutes, we've found that there's a trade-off. Many children will be less likely to look around and discover all the new rocks and sticks and streams if the familiar stuff is right in front of their face.

We choose to emphasize bikes, scooters, balls, and sidewalk chalk when it comes to packing play equipment. This way we know that they are more likely to be out enjoying the fresh air at the campground and also more likely to be interacting and making friends with the other kids.

4. **Give older kids a dedicated spot for all their stuff and a vessel to contain it.** As your kids get older, they're not going to be thrilled if you try to control every item that gets packed for a camping trip. We've had some pretty interesting items come along on family vacations, since we largely let the boys pack by themselves at this point. We control the chaos by giving them a very specific size of bag that they can fill with whatever they desire and then we show them a very specific place that it has to go in the camper.

5. **There's almost always a store where you can buy that thing you need.** This was one of those lightbulb moments for me. The epiphany came during that trip where all of my clothes got left at home. I was furious. Huffing and puffing and threatening to blow the whole camping trip down. But then I drove about ten minutes and bought some cute new articles of clothing. Years later, I still have a pair of sweatpants and a beach cover-up from that incident that I wear on a regular basis.

   On another trip, we discovered that one of our boys forgot to pack his bathing suit. This was at the beginning of my quest to form them into packing prodigies, and perhaps I had been a bit too confident. The problem was again solved with a very quick trip to a nearby big-box store. So yes, we try to keep a well-stocked camper and use our checklists, but honestly, it's no big deal if we forget something. It happens, and luckily for us, most camp stores sell paper towels.

6. **Pack for every weather contingency.** While we've cut back on various toys and gadgets over the years, I'm still a complete nut about being prepared for any and all weather events on a camping trip. It might be my natural aversion to being cold and wet or my many experiences with not having the right foul-weather gear over the years.

At this point, it doesn't matter what the weather forecast says. We are prepared with bathing suits, coats, rain jackets, and boots regardless. We always have sweatshirts for layering and hats for chilly mornings. Forty-two-degree days in Tampa, Florida, taught me some valuable lessons, and I became the mom who can always outfit her kids for the great outdoors. Once you spend a rainy day in an RV with three kids, you understand the value of a raincoat and rubber boots.

7. **Be prepared for minor and major medical and first aid situations while traveling.** I'll never forget the time we were heading down to Myrtle Beach and a camping friend of mine who had been there many times gave me her list of nearby hospitals and urgent care clinics. I was new to traveling with young kids and thought this was the weirdest information to pass along.

But after a year or so of experience, I understood completely. Kids get sick and hurt at home, and kids get sick and hurt when traveling. It just makes sense to be prepared with all those things you keep on hand in the medicine cabinet. We've become much more serious about having a well-equipped first aid setup, while also having the basics like Motrin, Benadryl, saline, and Pepto-Bismol.

In short, we found that we were usually traveling with way too much in the way of toys and clothes and way too little in the area of first aid supplies and foul-weather gear. It's worth it to be prepared for a spontaneous puddle-jumping session or unfortunate middle-of-the-night teething sessions. It's also worth it to leave the five bins of Legos at home.

Staying Organized

So how do you manage to be well prepared *and* stay organized? I'm not saying it's easy, and if you have the right temperament, it may be simpler just to embrace the mess. Unfortunately, I don't have that temperament. I hyperventilate when I feel surrounded by stuff that doesn't have a proper home, and that can happen in a split second when camping, whether in a tent, cabin, or RV. The rest of my family doesn't seem to be similarly affected, but they understand that we are all happier when Mommy isn't having a meltdown. So here are some of the ways we manage to stay organized in a tight space.

Packing Cubes

How do I love thee, sweet packing cubes? Let me count the ways. These little pouches are revolutionary, I promise. We have recommended them for years on our podcast—*The RV Atlas*—and on our blog, and we've received hundreds of messages from people who have fallen head over heels for them. They will completely transform your packing experience.

For the first few years of camping in our pop-up and travel trailer, we used the typical duffel bags or plastic bins for our clothes. This led to what I called the "rooting effect." I would pack all the folded clothes nice and neat for my family at the beginning of a trip, and after just one day, all the clothes would be a disorganized pile of messiness. Why? Because everyone had to root through the bags or bins to find that one shirt or pair of pants.

Packing cubes are small, zippered pouches that you can use to organize and separate your clothing to eliminate the rooting effect. Each one of my three boys has a color-coded set of three packing cubes. The first packing cube has socks, undies, and pj's; the second has T-shirts and long-sleeved shirts; the third has shorts and pants. The set of packing cubes stays at the end of their RV bunk beds, and they know exactly where to look to find each piece of clothing. They also know that the cubes have to be zipped up and stacked before they head out to play.

We now use these packing cubes when we're tent camping, cabin camping, or even flying to a vacation destination. I can put all three color-coded sets of packing cubes in a single duffle bag, and they know exactly whose is whose when we unpack at the destination. It's magic. Try it.

A Container for Everything

I have a friend who is a professional organizer, and one day she peeked into my RV cabinets and practically fainted. After recovering from her shock, she passed along an organizing secret that changed the future of my RV organization. Most RV cabinets are deep and provide plenty of space. The problem is lack of access, and things get cluttered and disorganized when you try to find something in the deep, dark abyss. My friend showed me that putting everything into a container was the answer to my storage issue. I also learned to use only square containers, as they fit better in standard cabinets. One container might have soap and body wash, while another would store the toothpaste and toothbrushes. It made it easy to reach in and remove just what you needed without knocking a bunch of stuff over and creating a mess.

This goes for those tent-camping bins that you keep stocked in the garage as well. Instead of having one giant bin full of all your gear, try breaking it up into smaller containers within the bin. I have all my cooking utensils in one pouch and kitchen gadgets like peelers and can openers in another.

Color-Code Everything

The first things I color-coded for the RV were those amazing packing cubes, and it was so helpful that I went on to color-code many of our camping supplies. Not only did I try to stick to designated colors for the boys' toothbrushes and water bottles, but I also applied the technique to our camping linens and towels. Knowing that all the camper sheets were navy and all the camper towels were gray helped me easily sort the laundry in the house and return everything to its proper place.

Create Small, Dedicated Bins

I adore the clear, plastic shoeboxes from The Container Store, because they help me stay organized and find things easily. Every year at the start of the camping season, I create a couple of bins of craft supplies and card games. I also use these shoeboxes to store our pet supplies, so I'm never without a leash or doggie bags. There's a bin for all of our first aid supplies and everyday vitamins and medicines. It's easy for me to grab this small stack of shoeboxes, whether we are going on a camping trip in the RV or to a cabin for the weekend.

Own Your Packing Personality

Whether you are a minimalist or the type of traveler who wants to bring along *all* the comforts of home, the key is to know your packing personality and create a system that helps you get out of the house and to the campground with minimal fuss. I have friends who actually pack individual outfits into ziplock bags to stay organized on camping trips. That kind of system would completely overwhelm me, but for them, it works perfectly.

The most effective strategy for me is making sure I get everything stocked in organized bins at the beginning of the camping season. Then I know I won't have to worry about paper towels, shampoo, and tinfoil for our upcoming getaways. In the end, our goal is to spend less time managing stuff and more time roasting marshmallows around the campfire.

Complete RV Stock-Up Checklist

Camp Furniture and Outdoor Gear

Think about how much time you want to spend setting up and breaking down camp. Some campers prefer to keep things simple, and others want all the comforts of home. Find your own personal style before blowing too much money on camp gear.

Must Have

- ☐ one camp chair per traveler
- ☐ outdoor rug/RV mat
- ☐ tablecloth
- ☐ tablecloth clips
- ☐ lanterns
- ☐ clothesline
- ☐ insect repellent (lanterns, candles, etc.)

Nice to Have

- ☐ awning lights
- ☐ folding table
- ☐ pop-up shelter
- ☐ Bluetooth speaker
- ☐ rope lights
- ☐ hammock
- ☐ cornhole set
- ☐ slackline
- ☐ fly swatter

RV Tools and Safety Gear

These items will often make or break your camping experience. Make sure you have the right tools when you need them!

Must Have

- ☐ wheel chocks
- ☐ extra boards for unhitching and leveling
- ☐ level
- ☐ sewer hose
- ☐ water hose

- ☐ tire-pressure gauge
- ☐ surge protector
- ☐ water-pressure regulator
- ☐ water filter
- ☐ air compressor
- ☐ extension cord
- ☐ fire extinguisher
- ☐ jumper cables

- ☐ four-way lug wrench
- ☐ socket set
- ☐ rechargeable flashlight
- ☐ replacement bulbs
- ☐ fuse replacement kit
- ☐ extra batteries
- ☐ bungee cords
- ☐ latex gloves

Nice to Have

- ☐ Andersen camper levelers
- ☐ retractable hose with spray nozzle
- ☐ propane gauge
- ☐ walkie-talkies

- ☐ portable waste tank
- ☐ electric space heater
- ☐ 50-amp to 30-amp adapter
- ☐ 30-amp to 20-amp adapter

Kitchen (Indoor and Outdoor)

We like to be able to cook indoors or outdoors, depending on the time of year and the weather.

Must Have

- ☐ dinner plates (one for every family member, plus two)
- ☐ bowls (one for every family member, plus two)
- ☐ cups
- ☐ mugs
- ☐ silverware (one set for every family member, plus two)
- ☐ nesting bowls
- ☐ cutting board
- ☐ quality knife set
- ☐ spatula
- ☐ stirring spoon
- ☐ slotted spoon
- ☐ ladle
- ☐ tongs
- ☐ peeler
- ☐ meat thermometer
- ☐ collapsible colander
- ☐ collapsible whisk
- ☐ measuring spoons
- ☐ measuring cups

- ☐ dish towels
- ☐ washcloths
- ☐ sponges
- ☐ pot holders
- ☐ dish-drying rack
- ☐ cast-iron skillet
- ☐ cast-iron Dutch oven
- ☐ pot with lid
- ☐ casserole dish
- ☐ baking pan
- ☐ coffee maker
- ☐ grill
- ☐ grill brush
- ☐ grill spatula
- ☐ grill tongs
- ☐ camp stove
- ☐ camp stove fuel
- ☐ can opener
- ☐ bottle opener
- ☐ kitchen scissors
- ☐ lighter

Nice to Have

- ☐ blender
- ☐ Instant Pot/slow cooker
- ☐ electric water kettle
- ☐ electric griddle
- ☐ coffee thermos
- ☐ pie irons
- ☐ roasting sticks
- ☐ ice maker
- ☐ cooler

First Aid

Many first aid and medicinal items are temperature-sensitive, so we keep them all in containers that can easily be transferred out of the camper when not in use.

Must Have

- ☐ prescription medications
- ☐ sunscreen
- ☐ bug spray
- ☐ bee sting kit
- ☐ burn ointment
- ☐ calamine lotion
- ☐ aloe
- ☐ pain reliever
- ☐ antibiotic ointment
- ☐ Benadryl
- ☐ Pepto-Bismol
- ☐ cough syrup
- ☐ hydrogen peroxide
- ☐ rubbing alcohol
- ☐ first aid kit
- ☐ waterproof first aid kit for excursions

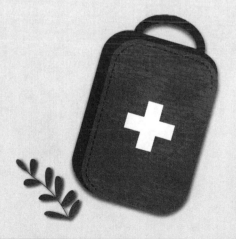

Bedrooms

We highly recommend having dedicated bedding for all the beds in the RV. Bringing pillows and blankets out to the RV every time you travel is for the birds! Some folks buy cheaper bedding to save money, but you will want to be as comfortable in the RV as you are at home.

Must Have

- ☐ pillows
- ☐ fitted sheets
- ☐ comforters
- ☐ extra sheets and blankets (two or three)
- ☐ packing cubes for clothing
- ☐ collapsible laundry hamper
- ☐ extra phone charger

Nice to Have

- ☐ mattress, upgraded
- ☐ mattress pad
- ☐ reading pillow
- ☐ reading light
- ☐ 3M hooks for jackets, coats, backpacks, and sweatshirts
- ☐ card and board games
- ☐ dedicated camper movies
- ☐ dedicated camper books

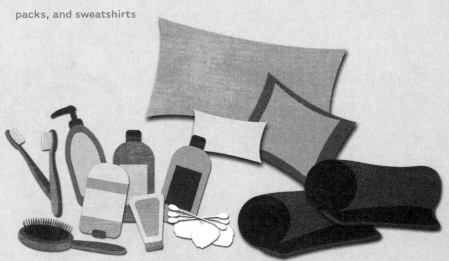

Bathroom

We stock the RV with all of our family toiletries at the beginning of the camping season each year. This way we never have to worry about forgetting that toothbrush!

Must Have

- ☐ shampoo
- ☐ conditioner
- ☐ body wash
- ☐ face cleanser
- ☐ body lotion
- ☐ face moisturizer
- ☐ toothbrush
- ☐ toothpaste
- ☐ dental floss
- ☐ deodorant
- ☐ hairbrush

- ☐ shaving razor
- ☐ shaving cream
- ☐ hand soap
- ☐ hand sanitizer
- ☐ cotton balls
- ☐ cotton swabs
- ☐ nail clippers
- ☐ bath towels
- ☐ washcloths
- ☐ hand towels
- ☐ garbage can

Nice to Have

- ☐ Oxygenics showerhead
- ☐ oil diffuser
- ☐ hair dryer

- ☐ bath mat
- ☐ extra towel hooks

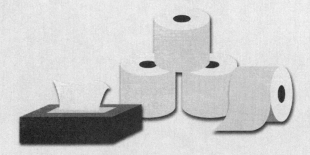

Consumables

These are items that you will have to restock throughout the camping season. Keep a dedicated note on your smartphone for any consumable supplies in the camper.

Must Have

- ☐ paper plates
- ☐ paper bowls
- ☐ plastic cups
- ☐ napkins
- ☐ paper towels
- ☐ toilet paper
- ☐ tissues

- ☐ trash bags
- ☐ heavy-duty tinfoil
- ☐ plastic wrap
- ☐ ziplock bags
- ☐ dish soap
- ☐ hand soap
- ☐ rubber gloves

Cleaning Supplies and Chemicals

Try to keep it simple and multifunctional when it comes to cleaning supplies in the RV. Be careful not to use abrasive chemicals and brushes without spot testing first! Also, be aware that bleach can wear down valves and seals, so use it with caution.

Must Have

- ☐ all-purpose spray
- ☐ window cleaner
- ☐ laundry detergent
- ☐ stain remover
- ☐ magic erasers
- ☐ baby wipes

- ☐ indoor broom
- ☐ outdoor broom
- ☐ waste tank chemicals
- ☐ water tank sanitizer
- ☐ awning cleaner

Nice to Have

- ☐ cordless vacuum

Sports and Recreation

Think about the recreational equipment that you will use on most of your RV trips and consider storing them in the camper permanently.

Must Have

- ☐ life jackets
- ☐ inflatable tubes
- ☐ whiffle ball and bat set
- ☐ basketball
- ☐ soccer ball
- ☐ kickball
- ☐ fishing poles
- ☐ tackle box
- ☐ fishing net

Pet Supplies

Traveling with your furry companions? Make sure you have all their supplies too!

Must Have

- ☐ food bowl
- ☐ water bowl
- ☐ extra leashes
- ☐ waste bags
- ☐ brush
- ☐ folder with copies of vaccinations and rabies certificate
- ☐ current photo
- ☐ dog bed/crate
- ☐ dog lead with stake or pen
- ☐ airtight container for food/treats

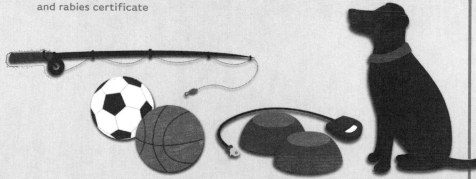

CHAPTER

Eight

BECOMING
a Weekend
WARRIOR

JEREMY

When we bought our first RV ten years ago, I was legitimately concerned that we wouldn't use it that much. I worried that it would gather dust in the driveway. After all, we live at the Jersey Shore in a boating community, and plenty of people buy boats that sit on cinder blocks in their driveways (or on their front lawns!) all summer long. Those boats look so sad to me—and when their owners walk past them, I imagine that they feel sad too.

I get it. Trust me, I do. Life gets busy, and our best intentions can get blasted by the nine-to-five grind. But Stephanie and I were determined to use our RV as much as possible.

So we did. We became weekend warriors.

Before we knew it, we were camping every other weekend in the spring and fall. Our busy work schedules didn't stop us; instead, they motivated us even more to get to the campground on the weekends. We discovered a handful of great campgrounds in New York, New Jersey, and Pennsylvania that we could reach in about two hours or less—and we went to them again and again.

We went camping on the weekends to relax, unwind, and have adventures in nature with our little boys. We wanted to escape that feeling of emptiness that you get on a Friday night after spending hours scrolling through your social media feeds. Those weekend RV trips fulfilled us, and they still do. Our family bond is strong because it has been forged by that time spent together, by setting up and breaking down camp—and by all of the fun stuff that happens in between. Our camping trips always bring us closer together as a family, and closer together is where we will stay.

We had a serious case of wanderlust back then, *and* a set of brand-new twin babies, *and* an unquenchable desire to get outside. But we also had jobs that we loved and cared about—and limited time for travel. Going to campgrounds that were relatively close to home may not have seemed like a grand adventure to us initially, but eventually we realized that we were having the time of our lives. We decided to define adventure on our own terms and nobody else's—and you should too.

You don't have to visit the Grand Canyon to have an amazing outdoor experience with your family—you just need to get outside. Because when you dip your toes in a river or feel a fish tugging on the line or feel the warmth of a campfire on your cheeks, it doesn't really matter where you are, as long as you're together.

We initially bought the RV for long trips to bucket-list destinations, but we soon realized that camping on the weekends could be just as fun. Once we spent our first weekend at a campground about two hours away from our house, we were completely hooked. And let's face it...weekend trips are a lot easier to pull off for working parents with busy kids!

As RV owners, we feel like adventure and escape are always within reach, even if only for two (or hopefully three) days at a time. The yin and yang of home and away has been deeply satisfying to us. Our children have deep roots in our community, but they have also experienced the life-changing joy of travel.

The push and pull of home and away are complementary forces in our minds, and that is most apparent to us when we take our weekend trips. We are so excited to leave on a Friday after school and work, but we are also happy to come home on a Sunday night—especially if we order in Chinese food after we unpack.

Over the years, we have nearly perfected how we prepare for, carry out, and return from our weekend warrior trips. Our family has become a well-oiled camping machine. We may be exhausted and burned out at 4:00 p.m. on a Friday afternoon—but by 8:00 p.m. on a Friday night, you know where to find us, right? You'll see us at the campground. That's for sure. We'll be relaxing around a warm, crackling campfire with Johnny Cash on the radio and burgers and corn on the grill.

Twelve Tips for Weekend Warriors

Are you also at a stage in life where you are working hard during the week but seeking adventure on the weekends? Do you want your kids to spend Saturday mornings climbing mountains instead of streaming Netflix? Then you are a perfect candidate for becoming a weekend warrior!

If you follow these twelve tips closely, I'm sure we'll see you at the campground too.

Tip #1: Embrace the Art of the Long Weekend

According to Project: Time Off, 52 percent of American workers do not use all of their vacation days. Collectively, these workers *are not using 705 million vacation days*—which is bad for their personal happiness and for the American economy. Are you one of those Americans leaving vacation time on the table because you are just too busy to get away? I understand that a weeklong vacation can be tough to pull off, but what about occasionally taking a long weekend? If you ask me, a three-day camping trip is twice as good as a two-day camping trip. The math may sound suspicious, but it's true! A traditional two-day weekend only gives you one full day at the campground. A three-day weekend gives you two full days at the campground!

Taking a three-day weekend also allows many of us to avoid weekend traffic and delays checking into a campground on a busy Friday evening. If you can get to a campground on a Thursday night, you can enjoy an empty campground Friday morning and afternoon, because most folks won't be showing up until evening. During these quiet hours at the campground, you can enjoy an empty pool or fishing spot—or just bask in the peace and quiet.

Tip #2: Reduce the Driving Distance

When we are taking the RV out for the weekend, departure and arrival times play a huge role in our planning. Friday evening rush-hour traffic can be a nightmare. If we show up too late to have a campfire, it really feels like a wasted night. Likewise, Sunday return traffic can be congested, and we always want to get home early enough to prepare for the week ahead. But at the same time, who wants to wake up on Sunday morning and have to pack up in a hurry and rush home just to unpack again?

Knowing that a campground is only one or two hours away relieves much of that travel stress. You can leave after work on Friday afternoon and still be sitting around a campfire that evening. It's also easy to return home on Sunday afternoon and throw in a load of laundry or take a trip to the grocery store. A little less time on the road can mean a lot less stress in the scheduling department.

There are dozens of awesome campgrounds within a four-hour radius of our home that we would love to visit on a weekend trip, but we typically save them for longer trips and stick closer to home when we only have a weekend (hopefully a long one!) to get away. This may mean that we are returning to the same campgrounds for our weekend trips, but that doesn't bother us. We know that there will be plenty of time to explore new places in the summer, and we love returning to familiar places that fit us perfectly, like a pair of old jeans

We have our weekend warrior campgrounds wired. We know the best sites and best seasons to visit each of them. During busy holiday and summer weekends, we also make sure to head in the opposite direction of traffic. For us, that means driving west and visiting eastern Pennsylvania instead of driving north and heading to the Catskills or Adirondacks in New York State.

Tip #3: Camp *Really* Close to Home on Busy Weekends

Sometimes even a two-hour drive is too far away! Once our boys started to participate in organized sports, unscheduled weekends became a distant memory. Add in birthday parties, graduations, and family barbecues, and we began to wonder how we would ever fit in our next camping trip!

Camping really close to home (as in, thirty minutes or less) means that our family can still attend sports games or family functions *and* squeeze in some valuable campground time. We set up the RV on Friday evening and unwind around the campfire, then head off to a baseball game the next morning. By Saturday afternoon, we are back at the campground fishing and playing catch.

It took us years to discover the pleasures of camping really close to home. Now, every spring, we look forward to sitting down with our family calendar and setting aside weekends where we will enjoy quick, simple getaways practically in our own backyard. Give it a try, and it may become a favorite part of your RV experience too. It sure beats giving up camping entirely when your kids start playing sports.

It's also a pretty crafty way to camp for several other reasons.

Parents know that just when you think you have everything down, something changes. We have loved the way that camping close to home has allowed us to see if our little guy really is ready to move from the Pack 'n Play into the bottom bunk, or if we will be able to stagger bedtimes for the kids at night.

You can also test out that new solar panel setup or tankless water heater. If something doesn't work, you are just a few miles away from home, where a hot shower awaits. Did you just get new tents, kayaks, or bike racks or install a weight-distribution system? There is no better way to test out new gear than by taking a short drive to a familiar campground.

Many RV experts recommend testing out all your RV systems after a long winter of sitting in the driveway. It took us awhile to realize the value of a season-opener trip really close to home, where we could dewinterize, easily replace a blown fuse or light bulb, and stock up on necessary supplies. Now we can dewinterize in a risk-free environment.

Booking a nearby camping weekend in early spring devoted to getting the RV into tip-top shape for the season is always a wise move. It's like our version of spring-cleaning, but we get to sit around the cozy campfire at night!

Tip #4: Become a Tourist in Your Own Backyard

We all know the story of having great activities, festivals, and parks in our hometowns that we never get around to enjoying. Real life gets in the way, and sometimes our weekends can be consumed by playing catch-up on chores, errands, and yard work or, heaven forbid, just catching up on the bills.

Camping close to home (or really close to home!) takes us away from the demands of daily life and encourages us to look at our area through the eyes of a traveler. What would we do if we were visiting this region for the first time? Where would we eat? Getting away from the busyness of our everyday lives helps us to enjoy our home even more.

We have lived at the Jersey Shore (near New York City and Philadelphia) for years, and sometimes we forget just how much there is to do right in our extended backyards. But this past fall, we spent a weekend camping near Philadelphia and rediscovered our love for this great American city, for its history and cheesesteaks! We could go into Philly anytime, but we rarely do. Why? Because we take it for granted, that's why. But when we camped right outside of Philly at a KOA recently, we felt like tourists again, and we couldn't wait to head into town on Saturday morning. The only question for us was, "Whiz, wit or witout?"

> Fifty-four percent of campers travel less than one hundred miles from home to camp.
>
> *(KOA, 2019 North American Camping Report)*

Tip #5: Consider Reserving a Seasonal RV Site

If your vacation time is limited because of work or family obligations, then you might consider renting a seasonal site at a nearby campground. When you rent a seasonal site, you set up your RV in early spring (or whenever the campground opens for the season) and keep it there until the campground closes in late fall or early winter. Depending on the local climate and a campground's seasonal rules, you may be able to keep your RV on the same site all year long.

The benefits of seasonal camping are many. You don't need to hitch up your RV each weekend to go camping because it's already set up and waiting for you. At the end of each weekend, you don't need to tow your rig home either. You set up your site one time for the entire season and then pack it all up at the end. When you pull into the campground each Friday, your chairs will be set up and your grill and camp kitchen will already be in place. Less work means more relaxation, and seasonal sites are significantly less work than visiting different campgrounds each weekend.

RV owners with a serious case of wanderlust may not want to spend every weekend in the same place, but sometimes, for some people, it really can make sense. Renting a seasonal site also doesn't have to be a permanent decision. It may make sense to stay put one year and then travel the next. Work and family obligations can get tricky fast, so it's nice to have as many options as possible when it comes to spending time at the campground. A seasonal site may also be perfect for couples with different work and vacation schedules. If one parent has the weekend off but the other doesn't, the kids can still go camping.

Prices for seasonal sites vary widely in our neck of the woods, with basic campgrounds charging $3,000 and up and some resort campgrounds charging well over $5,000 for the year.

We were seasonal campers a few years back, for just one year. We loved it for all of the reasons mentioned above. But our wanderlust got the better of us. We gave up our seasonal site after a year for the allure of the open road, but I still miss pulling into the campground on a Friday night and having our RV all set up and ready to go.

Tip #6: Prepare throughout the Week

While weekend camping trips can be incredibly relaxing and rejuvenating, packing for them is not. Waiting until the last second to pack for such a short trip can be chaotic and stressful. Imagine your kids desperately searching for sneakers, bathing suits, and baseball gloves after school on a Friday afternoon while Dad honks the horn in the driveway, and you'll get the picture.

That's why we start packing early in the week in small fifteen- to thirty-minute chunks. It works like a charm for us and eliminates all kinds of stress on Thursday nights and Friday afternoons. We start by packing bedding and linens on Tuesday nights, clothing on Wednesday nights, and food on Thursday nights. I also hitch up the RV on Thursday night and pull it in front of the house so that we're ready to leave the second I get home from work on Friday. These time-saving strategies often help us get on the road before rush-hour traffic really kicks into high gear.

Getting your own packing routine down is essential for anyone who wants to become a weekend warrior. If packing is too stressful, you might eventually prefer to spend your weekends at home. But if you can master the art of packing for a weekend trip, you will spend many happy weekends at the campground making memories with family and friends. You will want to return again and again.

Tip #7: Have a Set Weekend Menu and Shopping List

Disorganized food prep, or a complete lack of food prep, can also make a weekend camping trip stressful—especially when hungry kids are involved. So what's your goal: to keep it simple or to set up a full-blown camp kitchen? We always ask ourselves this question before a trip. If we are camping close to home at a state park and the whole point of the weekend is just to chill out and enjoy the campground, then we might go a little crazy and plan some elaborate meals.

On weekends like this, we'll make a huge breakfast with pancakes, eggs, and bacon on our Blackstone griddle, and we might use pie irons to make pizza over the campfire in the evening. But if we are taking a weeklong vacation in a place like Charleston or Cape Cod, then we might keep the food really simple, so that we have more time to explore and eat great local food. For these types of trips, we will pack cold cuts, PB&J, and cold cereal or oatmeal for the morning, so that we can get out the door and start exploring as quickly as possible.

No matter what kind of trip you are planning, having a set menu is absolutely key—especially for those quick weekend trips. We hate waking up at the campground and not knowing what we are feeding the kids, because they absolutely drive us crazy when there is any uncertainty about what they are going to eat.

Tip #8: Find Your Favorite Grocery-Store Hack

The most important part of preplanning a weekend camping trip is probably the grocery shopping and food prep. It can also be the most cumbersome and time-consuming, if you don't do it right. Over the years, we have developed several "grocery-store hacks" that really help us get to the campground and get home with minimal stress. Stephanie often goes to the grocery store on Thursday night and does her shopping for the upcoming weekend of camping *and for the entire following week*. Coming home to empty cupboards after a fun weekend is a total bummer! Who wants to go grocery shopping again on a Sunday night? Not us.

We have also experimented with meal-delivery services such as HelloFresh, Dinnerly, and Home Chef. These services are awesome for super-busy workweeks when it's a challenge just to get to the grocery store. Sometimes we have meals delivered on a Wednesday or Thursday for a camping trip, and sometimes we have them delivered Sunday night for the week ahead.

Grocery-shopping services online can also help you save time during the week and get to the campground with less stress. We have used

AmazonFresh, Instacart, and Walmart's grocery-delivery service, so that we can skip a trip to the grocery store and use that time to pack up our bikes and kayaks. It can also be a big relief to have your groceries delivered on a Sunday night if you didn't get to the store before camping that weekend.

Tip #9: Order Takeout for Friday Supper at the Campground

If we really have a frantic workweek before a camping weekend, we occasionally get takeout on Friday night on our way to the campground. It's no fun showing up at 8:00 p.m. on a Friday night and having to cook for hangry kids, so if we are going to get in late, we often grab subs at Jersey Mike's and call it a day. Letting the boys eat in the back seat of my truck used to stress me out, but they beat that out of me very quickly. Worrying about keeping things "nice" with three little boys is an exercise in futility.

So we choose our battles. We hope you choose yours too.

Depending on the timing of our arrival, we also might grab takeout near the campground. This requires a bit of advance planning and local knowledge, because you need to be certain that there is somewhere to park your rig while you run in to grab the grub.

Many campgrounds also have local pizza shops that will deliver right to your site. This can be an absolute lifesaver. I must admit, it is pretty awesome to pull into a campground and find the delivery person waiting at your site with hot food. The timing can be tricky, but we usually get it right. Call the campground ahead of time and ask them about your options for food delivery. If there are ten options, ask them where they like to order from when they get hungry! You'll always get the best recommendation.

Tip #10: Splurge for a Late Checkout on Sunday

As mentioned, we like to extend our camping weekends by staying three nights instead of two. But when we can't do that, we like to splurge for a late checkout on Sunday. If another camper hasn't reserved your site for Sunday (or any day), campground owners will often let you check out late for a small fee. We have payed anywhere from $5 to $20 for a late checkout, and we are often pleasantly surprised to find that some campgrounds let you stay late for free. Especially if you ask nicely!

Tip #11: Invite Friends and Family to Camp with You

True confession: sometimes when we camp close to home, we are not exactly camping in the most exciting places. We have a local county park that Stephanie and I both love, but the boys only love it under certain conditions. If we camp at this little campground all alone, with just our family, it's kind of a yawn for our three sons. So how do we make this campground exciting for them? We invite other families with kids to come.

Boom!

All of a sudden, camping here is just as exciting as camping at Disney World, at least for our three boys. They love camping with their buddies, and they can entertain themselves for hours when they are together at the campground. While the boys occupy themselves with their friends, Stephanie and I get time to chat with the other parents and relax around the campfire. We also get more time for reading, cooking, relaxing, and, *god forbid*, maybe even taking a nap!

Tip #12: Enforce SWAT Team Sunday

Successful weekend warriors must get their packing and food-prep game down to a science. But they also have to become masters of quick and efficient unpacking. As Stephanie explained in the previous chapter, when we get home from a weekend of camping, we call our unpacking routine SWAT Team Sunday. The entire family must chip in and help before anyone can sit down! We unload the camper, empty the RV fridge, and restock our house fridge. Then we get all of the dirty laundry into the washing machine, give the RV and truck a quick vacuum, and call it a day. If the kids help out according to our expectations, we order takeout and let them pick a Netflix movie. When we have spent the entire weekend outdoors, we have no problem getting our Pixar fix on come Sunday night.

SWAT Team Sunday is absolutely essential if you want to be a weekend warrior, because leaving the camper messy after a camping trip will make your next camping trip miserable. You will have to clean up and pack all at once, and who wants to do that?

It's hard to believe that ten years ago I spent time worrying about whether we would use the RV or not. I'm so glad that I didn't let those doubts get the best of me. Are you considering buying an RV but worrying that you won't use it enough? Then I would encourage you to make the plunge and join our happy tribe of weekend warriors. It might change your life for the better, much like it changed ours.

Clothing Packing List for the Weekend Warrior

You'll need a set of three color-coded packing cubes for each member of the family.

Kid Cube

For kids, make sure to pack for the number of days you will be traveling, plus one.

- ☐ three pairs of undies
- ☐ three pairs of socks
- ☐ three T-shirts
- ☐ three long-sleeved shirts
- ☐ three pairs of shorts
- ☐ three pairs of pants
- ☐ two pairs of pj's
- ☐ one sweatshirt
- ☐ sneakers and slip-ons/UGGs/Crocs

Mom Cube

- ☐ exercise clothing (leggings, two T-shirts, socks, sneakers)
- ☐ comfy morning/evening clothes (sweatpants, leggings, long-sleeved T-shirt, sweatshirt)
- ☐ pajamas
- ☐ two pairs of jeans and one pair of hiking pants
- ☐ three shirts that can be matched with pants
- ☐ undergarments
- ☐ shoes (hiking shoes, slip-ons)

Dad Cube

- ☐ exercise clothing (shorts, two T-shirts, socks, sneakers)
- ☐ three pairs of shorts
- ☐ one pair of jeans
- ☐ two pairs of hiking pants
- ☐ three shirts
- ☐ two sweatshirts
- ☐ undergarments
- ☐ shoes (hiking shoes, sandals)

Always Stocked in the Camper

- ☐ rain jackets
- ☐ hiking backpacks
- ☐ slippers
- ☐ flip-flops
- ☐ hats
- ☐ extra sweatshirts

EXIT 24B

CAMPGROUND

J eremy and I have always loved a good road trip. Even before we started traveling together, we rarely boarded planes. Jeremy would pile into a car with his buddies and head south in search of great surf breaks. When I was sixteen, I took an Amtrak train across the country from Philadelphia to Portland and spent most of my time in the observation car, staring in wonder as the Badlands and Glacier National Park passed by outside the windows.

Slow travel got ahold of us early on, and we never shook it off. In fact, that's why we started shopping for an RV in the first place. Road trips were still our favorite kind of travel, but they became a heck of a lot more complicated once kids came into the picture. After becoming parents, we still wanted to drive to amazing destinations, watching the landscape gradually change and discovering hidden treasures along the way. But we also wanted to make the journey easier and a lot more comfortable.

It turns out that traveling with an RV and staying at campgrounds along the way did in fact make all of our family road-tripping dreams come true. We've visited dozens of states with our kids and have taken the time to soak up the beauty and culture of each place. Our boys know that they can find the best hush puppies at roadside diners in the South. They know that you should never pass a Buc-ee's in Texas without stopping for a taco and a bag of Beaver Nuggets. And they know the wonder of watching the towering coastal dunes in Oregon fade away as the giant redwoods of Northern California come into view.

That's not to say that our road trips have been one magical moment after another. Jeremy and I have uttered classic parenting lines ("Don't make me turn this car around!") more times than we would care to admit. We never claim that having big adventures with kids is easy. The real question is... Is it worth it?

And our unequivocal answer, after a decade of experience, is a resounding yes. Yes, yes, *yes*!

Put your kids in the car and go on road trips. As much as possible. Stop at campgrounds along the way. There will be tears. There will be fighting. There will be endless rounds of "he's looking at me" emanating from the back seat.

But there will also be singing and laughing and memory-making that will carry your family through even the most difficult times in the future. We know that our kids will remember the Corn Palace and Wall Drug Store and all those other wacky roadside stops in South Dakota for decades. One day they'll bore their own kids to tears with stories about how every single member of our family got a stomach bug on the long drive back from Mount Rushmore to New Jersey and ended up puking in at least five different states. And, like magic, the worst parts of the trip will become the funniest memories that make up the story of our family.

One road trip at a time.

Why Is Slow Travel So Important to Us?

We do travel on airplanes with our kids once or twice a year. Sometimes that bucket-list destination—the Pacific Northwest or Texas Hill Country—is just too far for us to drive during a weeklong break from school. We stay in campgrounds even on these "fly-and-drive" family vacations, and we still have an amazing time together exploring new places.

Nevertheless, road trips provide our family with some opportunities that we miss out on with fast travel. The older our kids get, the more we appreciate all that quality time we've clocked in the family car, learning about each other and the beautiful world passing by outside our windows. There are, without a doubt, tricky parts of being stuck in an automobile with kids for long periods of time, but here are the four reasons why slow travel is so important to us as parents.

1. **Road trips give our kids the opportunity to be bored.** I know, I know...This doesn't sound like a perk. But experts keep telling us that our fast-paced culture is robbing kids of the creativity and thoughtfulness that comes from sheer boredom. And even though we do our best to provide unscheduled downtime for the family, our boys still treat us like their own personal camp counselors. They are used to having a full slate of activities, sports, and playdates. When things slow down a bit, they often just look for the TV remote and plop down on the couch until it's time for the next organized activity.

   The good and bad news is that there's no escaping the boredom of a long road trip. Hours pass by, and it's up to us to find ways to entertain ourselves. It's not a piece of cake to force your kids to be bored, but we believe that it's an incredibly important part of raising creative and thoughtful humans. So we appreciate that road trips help us do just that.

2 **Road trips encourage us to find entertainment that we can all enjoy together.** When many of us were kids, there was only one television in the house, and we all had to agree on the shows we watched. I still remember watching the sitcom *ALF* with my family every Monday night at 8:00 p.m. I love having shared entertainment experiences with my kids, and I embrace the challenge of finding music, podcasts, games, and audiobooks that we can all enjoy together. It's definitely not an easy task, but it's always worth it to me. At the end of every summer, I compile a music playlist with our favorite family jams. Those are some of my very favorite "souvenirs" from our road trips.

3 **Road trips help our kids learn about regional cultures and geography in real time and in relation to where they live.** Our boys have grown up learning about this country by looking out the windows of our family car. They know what it's like to drive across the Appalachian Mountains, the plains of Ohio, and the shores of the Great Lakes before arriving in the Badlands of South Dakota. The experience of piecing these regions together in real time is something you just can't mimic when you fly to a destination. Our kids learned all their states by playing license-plate bingo for years in the back seat. They have tracked our trip progress in kid-friendly road atlases. And they've seen how landscapes, weather, roads, and architecture change as we drive along.

4 **Road trips encourage kids to enjoy the journey and connect dreamy destinations with interesting stops along the way.** It's impossible for us to drive very far without needing a pit stop. Whenever we plan a road-trip route, we look for fun, interesting, or educational stops along the way. Many of these places wouldn't merit a trip all on their own, but since we are passing through, we take the time to pull over and check them out.

We've had some pretty amazing experiences arise out of these pit stops. Mount Airy, North Carolina (Andy Griffith's hometown), ended up being one of our family's funniest memories of all time. We took a tour in one of the Mayberry squad cars, and it broke down, leaving us stranded outside of Andy Griffith's childhood home. The boys still talk about that years later.

Screen Time: The Elephant in the Car

The topic of screen time is a tricky one to tackle, mostly because we are not in the business of telling other folks how to parent. However, managing screen time has been one of the most difficult things we've had to do as parents, and we know we're not alone in feeling that way. So we figure that it's important to talk about the decisions we have made and what has worked for us over the years.

Jeremy and I are both teachers by training, and we've seen all the research on the effects of too much screen time. We've also personally witnessed the impact of growing amounts of screen time on our students over the years, including lack of focus and decreased physical activity. We take the research seriously enough that our kids occasionally moan and groan about how unfair we are compared to all the other parents in the world. But in reality, we aren't super strict. The boys see most of the latest movies and can tell you about whatever ridiculous show is popular on Nickelodeon right now.

The truth is that we're members of the first generation of parents to have to navigate screen-time limits while traveling. When we were kids, a road trip meant leaving the television and VCR at home. Now that we have TVs in the car and endless entertainment options on our personal devices, we get the unwelcome responsibility of dealing with screen-time debates on vacation as well.

Admittedly, this technology makes some parts of travel much, much easier. I'm not above using screens strategically throughout the day to make a long drive more enjoyable for everyone. I'm also not above throwing my phone into the back seat on hour nine of a trip and telling the kids to just find something to watch and be quiet. But we also feel very deeply as parents that this easy fix can wipe out all the good things we are trying to accomplish by road-tripping with our kids.

So, like most difficult parenting issues, we've tried to find a balance that works for us. What that balance looks like has changed throughout the years with different ages, but here's a general overview. When our boys were very young (up until about age four), we didn't use any screen entertainment while traveling in the car. To be quite honest, this was not the easiest route to go, but we strongly believe that the effort paid off in spades. Now that they are older, our boys can travel for fairly long periods of time without asking for digital entertainment. They understand that there are other ways to keep busy on long car rides.

Once the kids were a bit older, we started introducing limited and strategic screen entertainment on longer car rides. We would bring along a DVD of their favorite cartoons and tell them what the "showtimes" would be. Nowadays, they might get two movies on my laptop (one at 10:00 a.m. and one at 3:00 p.m.) if we are driving ten hours in a day. That way we get a break from managing the kids throughout the day ("Are we there yet?" and "He's looking at me..." and so on), but there's still time for music, conversation, and maybe a podcast or audiobook.

One thing that we have remained firm on is no personal devices in the car on road trips. This will probably change as they enter their teen years, but for now we are sticking to our guns. A few years ago, the boys received iPods for Christmas, and we were open to letting them use them in the car while traveling. Unfortunately, that was more trouble than it was worth. The kids ended up having screen-time battles with us that we had never faced before. Plus, the iPods were an issue throughout the entire family vacation.

Two-thirds of teens claim that, even if they could not stay in touch via a smartphone or computer, they would still want to go camping.

(KOA, 2019 North American Camping Report)

We weighed our options and decided that we were okay with being labeled as the worst parents ever by our children. Currently, when we go on family vacations, the iPods stay at home. And regardless of how our kids feel, we are so much happier that way as parents. Thankfully, they only complain about this policy before we leave. Once we pull out of the driveway, their enthusiasm for the trip takes over, and it's like those iPods don't even exist.

By sharing our own decisions about screen time, we aren't trying to communicate that ours is the "right" or "better" way. We simply hope our experiences can help if you are struggling to set limits and establish some guidelines with your own kids. In the end, you have to find your own balance and decide what works for you as a family. These are not easy issues to navigate, and unfortunately, we are the first generation of parents to travel this road. We wish you Godspeed.

Road-Trip Gear

Must Have

- [ ] up-to-date registration
- [ ] RV insurance
- [ ] extra set of RV keys
- [ ] jumper cables
- [ ] emergency flare
- [ ] USB rechargeable flashlight
- [ ] road atlas

Nice to Have

- [ ] RV GPS
- [ ] OverDrive or Libby apps
- [ ] Allstays app
- [ ] audiobooks
- [ ] SiriusXM satellite radio

Before You Hit the Road

Often when we talk about a road trip, our focus tends to be on the actual car ride. But successful vacations start with good planning and preparation, so it's important to get your ducks in a row before hitting the road. These are the items on our personal to-do list when we head out for a one- or two-week family vacation in the summer. Of course, if you're only heading out for a long weekend, most of these tasks will be unnecessary.

Research Your Route in Advance

We are so used to having GPS on our smartphones that many of us forget to do advance scouting on driving routes. That's a mistake for more than one reason. First of all, we've traveled enough to discover that there are still places in America where you might not be able to get cell service. We've had connectivity trouble quite a few times when relying on our phones for navigation, especially in mountainous regions. We've also found that satellite GPS sometimes has the wrong location information for places like state and national park campgrounds. We have ended up at random administrative office buildings more than once before finally learning our lesson.

So what's the solution? Some navigation apps allow you to save or download routes, so that you can access them offline. It's also helpful to have a good old-fashioned printout of your route for reference in a pinch. We like to have a full arsenal of navigation tools at our disposal, so we travel with a printed route, an up-to-date road atlas, a few navigation apps on our smartphones, and a standard GPS. It sounds like overkill, perhaps. But have you ever tried to get a cell signal in the California redwoods?

If you are driving or towing an RV, you'll also want to avoid any routes with applicable height or weight restrictions. You can do your research in advance using Good Sam Club's online trip-planner tool, which offers filters for low clearance and tunnel restrictions. Some folks use truck atlases to avoid ending up on roads where RVs are prohibited, as they are on all New York State parkways. There are also GPS systems and navigation apps available that allow drivers to enter the height and width of their rig to avoid restricted roads, tunnels, and low overpasses.

Treat Your Vehicle to a Tune-Up

Make sure that all of your routine maintenance has been checked off before you head out on a road trip. Years ago, we started getting our annual automotive tune-up in late May or early June, since we do most of our road-tripping during the summer months. We have a trusted mechanic who understands that we clock some serious miles on our family car and that our primary goal is not to be stranded in the middle of nowhere. We make sure to schedule an appointment far enough in advance of our first trip that it won't be a stress point if any work needs to be done.

------ **Departure Checklist** ------

- ☐ Park one of your cars in the driveway.
- ☐ Put one light in your house on a timer.
- ☐ Make sure an outside motion-sensor floodlight is on.
- ☐ Unplug small appliances (toaster, coffee maker, television, etc.).
- ☐ Turn your water heater down.
- ☐ Set the thermostat to a seasonal temperature (we choose low eighties in the summer).
- ☐ Clean out the refrigerator and pantry.
- ☐ Take out all the trash.
- ☐ Make sure every toilet is flushed (a must if you have children!).
- ☐ Double-check smoke detectors and carbon-monoxide alarms.
- ☐ Double-check all registration, insurance, and driver's license documents.
- ☐ Do a last-minute walk around the property, checking all doors and windows.

Get Your Paperwork in Order

We've all forgotten to put that new registration or insurance card in the car at some point in the past. That's not the end of the world if you are going around the corner to the grocery store, but you do not want to end up hundreds of miles away from home without your vehicle documentation. We double-check that our registration and insurance cards are up to date and our E-ZPass account is funded for tolls. We also make sure that our roadside emergency membership is active.

Avoiding Common Pain Points on a Family Road Trip

Even though we have been road-tripping with our kids since they were infants, we still deal with all of the clichéd bad behavior in the back seat. Our boys get into ridiculous arguments about who is poking whom. They slip into verbal loops where they are asking us about our ETA every six seconds. Our experience has taught us, however, that many of the decisions we make as parents can either maximize or minimize the naughty behavior. When Jeremy and I are at our best as road-trip warriors, hours in the car pass much more smoothly. We don't always have our A game going when we hit the road, and we see the difference immediately. Here are some of the ways that we keep family road trips from becoming never-ending nightmares.

Develop a Car Routine

As a former teacher, I have a tendency to believe that routines are the answer to most of life's problems. This has definitely proven to be the case for road-tripping with our kids. When our boys have a general idea of what to expect and when to expect it, they tend to keep the verbal badgering and physical antics to a minimum.

So how do you create a routine over the course of endless hours in a car? I basically take all of the activities that are currently entertaining for our family and decide an order in which they will happen. Our family can usually last four hours in the car without a gas stop or bathroom break. I develop a general game plan for those four hours and then rinse and repeat after a rest stop. I try to alternate between quiet activities and more interactive ones. And yes, I try to control the incessant flow of snacks. This is how four hours might look right now for our family of school-aged kids:

-⟫ **20 minutes:** activity books with crossword puzzles or word searches

-⟫ **20 minutes:** family Mad Libs

-⟫ **20 minutes:** family-friendly podcast

-⟫ **20 minutes:** snack time

-⟫ **20 minutes:** game (alphabet game, license-plate game, 5 Second Rule, trivia)

-⟫ **20 minutes:** family-friendly audiobook

-⟫ **120 minutes:** *movie!*

Note that I always save the screen time for the last stretch, since they are bound to be more antsy then. These times are also super flexible and just one example of our many routines. If a game or podcast is holding their attention, I'll milk it for as long as possible.

Keep the Activities Low Prep and High Interest

When our twins were toddlers, I started poking around on Pinterest for road-trip activities. So many of the ideas seemed amazing in theory but demanded a ridiculous amount of advance preparation. As a busy mom, I didn't have the luxury of preparing for road trips weeks in advance. Also, some required purchasing a lot of cheap trinkets, and personally I would rather spend my money on a million things other than building a dollar store "road-trip treasure chest." I did take some time to make a binder of activities that I knew they could use over and over again. I put all the activity pages in clear protective sleeves along with a dry-erase marker and a sock for an eraser. These binders have lasted for years, and as the kids get older, I just swap out the printables with age-appropriate activities.

Another one of their favorite activities over the years has been those handheld water games that were a big hit in the 1980s. Remember those from the dentist's office? In an inspired moment, I bought a few of them online, and they became a staple for family road trips.

Apps for Road Trips

iExit
iExit integrates two popular resources: GasBuddy and Yelp. Getting gas can be a stressful endeavor when traveling with an RV, and this resource will help tremendously. You can access all nearby gas options, find the lowest price, and specifically hunt for diesel. There are also crowdsourced photos that can help you determine whether you can easily navigate the pumps.

Pilot Flying J
Pilot/Flying J gas stations tend to be RV friendly, so we use their Pilot Flying J app to locate nearby locations during our travels. If you are a member of the Good Sam Club, you can also take advantage of a gas discount using your membership card. Some locations have specific RV services like dump stations, propane fueling, and overnight parking. You can use the app to search out these stops.

USA Rest Stops
USA Rest Stops is a personal favorite that we have used for years. It's great for locating stops along your drive that are RV friendly. You can search by state and by route. We particularly appreciate this app when we are looking for a nice rest stop where we can have lunch in the RV (or at a picnic table) and let the kids stretch their legs.

CAT Scale Locator
Have you weighed your RV lately? Or ever? Every responsible RV owner needs to see what their RV *really* weighs when it's fully loaded for travel. It doesn't take long or cost that much, but it will guarantee that you are traveling within the weight limits of your rig and tow vehicle.

NOAA Hi-Def Radar

This weather app was recommended to us by someone who works at out-door festivals for a living. So we splurged on the $1.99 cost and down-loaded it. We've used it hundreds of times since then while camping.

Blue Beacon Truck Wash Locator

This app comes through in the clutch for anyone who needs to give their RV a bath before or after a vacation. We can't guarantee that there will be a Blue Beacon Truck Wash right near you, but at least you won't go wandering around in search of one!

Other RV Travel Apps for the Road:

▷ GasBuddy

▷ Trucker Path

▷ Allstays Truck and Travel

▷ Allstays RV Dumps

▷ Allstays Rest Stops Plus

▷ CoPilot

Build Anticipation and Deliver a Payoff

Jeremy and I realized years ago that if we want our kids to buy into family road trips, we have to create excitement and deliver some pretty fabulous experiences. We want our boys to anticipate big fun when we all pile into the car for a camping trip. We talk about stops we will make and always try to have some cool roadside experience along the way. On the way to Mount Rushmore, we showed them pictures of the Corn Palace and Wall Drug. As a family, we counted the Wall Drug signs for hours before we got there (213!). Then we gave them a small allowance to have fun doing classic things like buying corn on the cob and a whoopee cushion.

We always want them to feel like the journey is an investment. Long drives lead us to amazing new destinations. That might mean a cool sight-seeing stop or it might just mean a campground with a pool at the end of every driving day. Whatever is appealing to your kids, make sure you reward them for being road warriors.

Stock Up on Healthy Food and Snacks

I joke that my kids act like I'm running a snack stand the entire time we are in the car. A lot of us tend to pack "treats" to keep the kids happy and stop the whining and complaining. It didn't take me long to realize that we were working against ourselves by giving the kids more sugar or junk food than they were used to and then strapping them in their car seats for hours. When the lightbulb went off, I started to focus on packing snacks and treats that wouldn't give everyone a sugar high or make us all feel sluggish and cranky. Our goal is to keep them fed and watered, but not jumpy and hyper.

Before we leave, I stock up on individually packaged snacks like trail mix, dried fruit, granola bars, crackers and cheese, crackers and peanut butter, and popcorn. I also pack grapes, apples, hummus and pretzels, and jerky. Depending on the personalities of your kids, it may work to divvy the snacks up ahead of time and let them serve themselves in the car. We also keep a cooler packed with flavored seltzers. This way we avoid sugary drinks at gas stations while still satisfying our craving for something more interesting than water.

Make sure you squirrel away a bag of these snacks for the car ride home. I've learned that lesson the hard way over the years.

Build Physical Activity into the Day

I wear an activity tracker, and it is amazing how sedentary you are on a road trip compared to a typical day at home. Seeing those numbers on my fitness app has made me more conscious of working physical activity into a driving day. That effort pays off with the kids' behavior as well, making them less likely to act up in the car.

One of the ways we up our activity level is to take our meal breaks at a rest stop instead of a service station. Many rest stops have picnic tables and nice open spaces for running and playing. We'll throw out a ball for the boys to kick around or play a few games of Mother May I and Simon Says. I've done simple obstacle courses, telling them to skip to the tree, walk around it five times, then hop back to the picnic table. We take our dog on a walk and do some stretches before getting back in the car. Whatever you do, squeeze as much movement as possible into those driving breaks.

Find Entertainment the Whole Family Enjoys

One of my very favorite road-trip challenges is finding entertainment that the whole family genuinely enjoys. We are always on the lookout for music, audiobooks, podcasts, and travel games that the kids will enjoy and that won't simultaneously bore us to tears.

MUSIC

Jeremy and I were never the type of parents to play official "kid music" in the car, so our boys grew up listening to our personal playlists. Now that they are older and have so many more opinions, we let all family members weigh in on the road-trip soundtrack. Satellite radio is a godsend for our family, and sometimes we do round-robin, letting each person choose a station for three songs. You can pick anything you want—Elvis, the Beatles, Hits 1, or Dance Hits—and no one is allowed to complain.

---------------------- **Road-Trip Mixtape** ----------------------

- "Don't Fence Me In": Bing Crosby and the Andrews Sisters
- "(Get Your Kicks on) Route 66": Nat King Cole
- "I've Been Everywhere": Johnny Cash
- "Carl Perkins' Cadillac": Drive-By Truckers
- "Every Day Is a Winding Road": Sheryl Crow
- "City of New Orleans": Willie Nelson
- "Take It Easy": The Eagles
- "Hey Jack Kerouac": 10,000 Maniacs
- "Another Travelin' Song": Bright Eyes
- "Mississippi": Bob Dylan
- "Car Wheels On a Gravel Road": Lucinda Williams
- "Take Me Home, Country Roads": John Denver
- "One Headlight": The Wallflowers

AUDIOBOOKS

Audiobooks were a surprise hit with our boys even when they were very young. I didn't think that they would be able to focus for long periods of time, but this is one of their favorite activities for longer car rides. We started with series like Harry Potter, Chronicles of Narnia, and I Survived. Now I consider it my own personal challenge to find a few new options before any trip. Audiobooks can be expensive, so check out the Libby or OverDrive apps. They connect to your local library and allow you to borrow books using your library card. Make sure to borrow and download the audiobooks before you hit the road. You'll probably need Wi-Fi for files that large.

----------- **Great Audiobooks for Kids of All Ages** -----------

- Magic Tree House
- Junie B. Jones
- My Weird School
- I Survived
- A to Z Mysteries
- The Genius Files
- How to Train Your Dragon
- Harry Potter
- Chronicles of Narnia

PODCASTS

Jeremy and I are huge podcast fans, but to be honest, most of our favorite shows are either not appropriate or not engaging for the whole family. It took some digging around, but we managed to compile a collection of podcasts that are fun or spark some interesting conversations. We are always on the lookout for new recommendations and have built a list of possibilities that will take us through their teenage years!

Podcasts for the Whole Family

- *Wow in the World*
- *Brains On!*
- *Good Night Stories for Rebel Girls*
- *Dream Big Podcast*
- *Story Pirates*
- *Tumble* (science podcast for kids)
- *The Alien Adventures of Finn Caspian* (science fiction)

TRAVEL GAMES

It's easy to forget what we all did for fun before we had endless entertainment on devices. I got into my own personal wayback machine and tried to remember the games that kept us entertained on long car rides when we were kids. It's not surprising to discover that simple things like the alphabet game, I Spy, and the license-plate game are pretty timeless. We've also reached out to other folks to learn new ones like Cows on My Side, which has now been a true family favorite for a couple of years. You get points for passing cows (or horses or anything else you decide) on your side of the car, but lose everything if you pass a graveyard.

Hard-Earned Road-Trip Wisdom

We love a good road trip, but even road warriors have their limits. Learn what works for your family and don't be afraid to set limits on how long you can spend in the car without losing your mind. We've learned that any more than two full days of driving just makes us all miserable. So we plan trips accordingly. If the destination is farther away than that, we break up the driving with additional stops, or we just fly.

We've also learned that driving at night is not a good fit for us. Countless people told us that's the way to roll with kids, so we tried it out a time or two. Our kids didn't sleep and we were wiped out. It didn't make anything easier, and we realized that just because other people do it doesn't mean that we have to. Be brave enough to try new things with your kids and be smart enough to stop if they don't work. The very best thing about road trips is turning the journey into your own personal adventure.

Time to Fuel Up!

Gas stops can be a big source of stress for newbie RVers. If you are driving or towing an RV, here are some of our tried-and-true tips.

Download the Pilot Flying J and iExit apps.
You won't always be near a Pilot Flying J, but the ones with RV lanes are literally the easiest way to get gas *ever*. Their RV lanes have both regular gas and diesel. In the Pilot Flying J app, you can search by your current location and see nearby options and the amenities at each particular stop. Otherwise, iExit will help you find the next-best gas option.

Look for gas stations where your rig will remain parallel to the road when you pull up to the pump.
We've found that staying parallel to the road allows for the easiest entry and exit at a service plaza. When you pull in at the angle that keeps you parallel to the road, go right through the gas lane closest to the road, and then pull out the other exit without any major turns.

Wait for your best gas lane.
Don't be nervous to wait in line for the easiest gas lane to open up. Even though your rig might be big, people can figure out how to get around you.

Use Google Earth to get a bird's-eye view of the gas stations ahead.
If you are a newbie and very anxious, this is the best way to calm your nerves and be confident about where you are fueling up.

Never pull in without a clear exit strategy.
If we cannot see a clear entry and exit, we simply do not pull in. We keep driving to the next service plaza. Getting yourself into a dead-end pickle is the worst-case scenario when towing.

Modern life is hectic and fast-paced for all of us. We live in a never-ending, 24/7 breaking-news cycle, and the news never seems to be good. Families are more divided over politics than ever before, and surviving Thanksgiving dinner may require therapy sessions both before and after the turkey is served. Our inboxes are also treacherous. They are exploding with so many emails that cleaning them out can feel a bit more like contending with a zombie apocalypse. Kill one email and another one pops up to take its place. Have you ever achieved inbox zero? I gave up a long time ago.

And then there's social media. There's a growing mountain of evidence that it actually makes us feel lonely and disconnected, yet none of us can seem to stop scrolling. Throw in the challenges of raising kids when both parents have to work to stay solvent, and things get crazy fast. It can make you feel like a hamster on a wheel.

I recently set up the screen-time feature on my phone to see just how much time I was spending staring at my phone every day. I was not happy with what I found. Not happy at all. So I worked hard to reduce my screen time and be more intentional about how I use my phone. I was also determined to set a good example for my kids. We can't expect them to be disciplined with their devices if we are not disciplined with ours. So I made some progress and cut down on my screen time. Then we went camping for a week.

At the end of the week, I was shocked to see my screen-time numbers. They were drastically reduced. I had barely picked up my phone that week. Instead of mindlessly scrolling through my social media feeds, I had spent hours of quality time with my wife and kids each day. We spent our days swimming and playing basketball and our nights relaxing around the campfire. It was downright therapeutic.

When we spend quality time together as a family around the campfire, time just seems to slow down. We shut off our devices and talk to our kids. We tell them stories and exchange jokes. We get to know them and they get to know us. They ask us questions about when we were kids, about how we met, and about what life was like before they were born.

Then, just when we couldn't love them any more, Stephanie and I put the little angels to bed so that we can spend some desperately needed time together around the campfire. Our three boys do not go gentle into that good night. In fact, they always burn and rave at the close of day. But they always fall asleep eventually.

Is your life hectic and hurried? Have you ever looked around your house only to realize that the ones you love most are all in separate rooms staring at screens? Then it's time to log into the original social network and discover your campfire mojo.

Here are the best tips and tricks to make it happen.

Nine Great Tips for Creating Campfire Mojo

Tip #1: Keep the Campfire Burning after the Kids Go to Bed

We like to build a family campfire before dinner and then spend a few hours chilling out with the kids. The boys love making s'mores and roasting hot dogs. Sometimes we even make our entire dinner over the campfire. But when it's time for the kids to go to bed, we keep the campfire burning. One of us will put the kids to bed while the other cleans up and monitors the campfire.

Once the rug rats are in bed, we have date night around the campfire. Stephanie will pour a glass of wine, and I will play some mellow music—SiriusXM Coffee House kind of music. Our days with the kids are heavy metal, so our nights have to be acoustic. Some of my happiest moments on this planet occur when the kids are snoozing away inside the cozy RV and Stephanie and I are reconnecting with each other under the architecture of moon and stars. We try to whisper. But sometimes we end up giggling over some absurd thing one of the boys said or did during the day. Some nights we stay up late until the campfire is nearly spent.

Tip #2: Buy Local Firewood That Is Well Seasoned (Not Green!)

On a more practical note, we are big believers in shopping locally, especially when it comes to buying firewood. The risks of transporting firewood from region to region are serious. According to the Environmental Protection Agency, exotic pests like the Asian long-horned beetle, emerald ash borer, and hemlock woolly adelgid have killed millions of trees in cities and forests across the country over the past fifteen years. Scary stuff, right? So please remember to leave your own firewood at home.

------------------ **Homemade Fire Starters** ------------------

Over the years, our boys have learned to build a pretty solid campfire.
They love making these fire starters before we head out for a fun camping
adventure.

1. Save your leftover toilet paper tubes.
2. Save your leftover dryer lint.
3. Stuff dryer lint into the toilet paper tubes.
4. Add orange peels or cinnamon sticks for an awesome campfire aroma!
5. Wrap the tube in newspaper.
6. Tie each end of the newspaper with twine.

You'll have no problem buying firewood at the campground. If it's too expensive, you can always purchase it nearby. Just make sure it's dry and well seasoned! Once, when my buddy Joe was about to buy firewood at a camp store in Maine, I told him that I had just bought firewood up the road that was half the price. A camp worker overheard me. She looked at me in disgust and said, "That firewood up the road is *green!*" Then she walked away. Joe and I used context clues to figure out that the cheap firewood up the road was not dry and well seasoned.

It turned out that the camp worker was right. The wood I had bought on the side of the road was still moist inside, and it did not burn nicely at all. We had a smoky campfire that night, and I felt like a silly little schoolboy. So much for saving three bucks. That's not even enough money to buy camp store ice cream these days.

Tip #3: Learn to Build a Proper Campfire

A proper campfire requires *tinder* (wadded-up newspaper, dryer lint, fire starters), *kindling* (small twigs and branches), and *fuel* (the well-seasoned firewood mentioned above). We use either the teepee method or the log cabin method, with a slight preference for the log cabin method, because it ends up being sturdier and less likely to topple over and throw sparks everywhere. Start with your tinder in the middle, then add kindling on top of the tinder pile. Then build your teepee or log cabin around the pile of tinder and kindling and light it up using a long match or a fire starter.

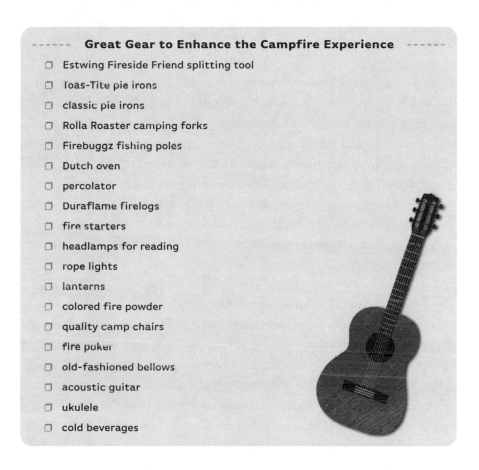

------- **Great Gear to Enhance the Campfire Experience** -------

- ☐ Estwing Fireside Friend splitting tool
- ☐ Toas-Tite pie irons
- ☐ classic pie irons
- ☐ Rolla Roaster camping forks
- ☐ Firebuggz fishing poles
- ☐ Dutch oven
- ☐ percolator
- ☐ Duraflame firelogs
- ☐ fire starters
- ☐ headlamps for reading
- ☐ rope lights
- ☐ lanterns
- ☐ colored fire powder
- ☐ quality camp chairs
- ☐ fire poker
- ☐ old-fashioned bellows
- ☐ acoustic guitar
- ☐ ukulele
- ☐ cold beverages

Just remember that thick pieces of firewood with lots of surface bark don't burn as nicely as thinner pieces. Most of the firewood that is sold at campgrounds needs some extra splitting. Use a splitting tool like the Fireside Friend by Estwing (not a traditional camp axe, which is not designed for splitting) to easily cut each piece of firewood into two smaller pieces. This will help you build an extra warm and toasty campfire. When you pull out your splitting tool at the campground, other campers will admire your skill and technique. Your fellow campers will look upon you as a modern-day Prometheus. By watching you, they will learn to make their own fires.

They will sing your name around their campfires for generations to come.

Tip #4: Be Strict about Proper Behavior around the Campfire

We absolutely expect that our kids will behave appropriately around the campfire. If they do not, it's off to bed for them! Stephanie and I set up a circle of chairs and tables around the fire, and we do not allow our kids to mess around inside that magic circle. No running is allowed inside the magic circle. No roughhousing is allowed inside the magic circle. And there is no throwing garbage or glass into the campfire. Ever.

Thankfully, none of our kids has ever tripped and fallen into an active firepit. Young Wes did once trip and fall into an unlit firepit, and that was painful enough.

Tip #5: Get Social around the Campfire

We love camping with other families and sharing meals and campfires with them. But if we are camping alone, we don't let that stop us from meeting new people and making new friends. Stephanie and I are not exactly extroverts, but campground culture brings out our social side. We often end up chatting with folks at neighboring sites or other parents at the pool and playground. Inviting them over to our camper might seem weird, but inviting them over for a campfire is not weird at all!

The secret to making fast friends at the campground is to practice the fine art of casual conversation and to keep it about positive topics like the ones mentioned above. We do not talk about politics or religion around the campfire, especially with people we are just getting to know.

The campground experience is all about finding and sharing common ground conversationally. If someone wants to debate politics or talk about divisive issues, there are a hundred other places to do so in our culture. For us, it's not about censorship; it's about respecting each other's right to relax and enjoy life away from all of that crap. When I'm sitting around a campfire, I don't even want to talk about politics with people who agree with me.

Campfire Mixtape

- "Ring of Fire": Johnny Cash
- "Fire It Up": Modest Mouse
- "Instant Karma": John Lennon
- "Champagne Supernova": Oasis
- "Burning Love": Elvis Presley
- "Light My Fire": The Doors
- "Norwegian Wood (This Bird Has Flown)": The Beatles
- "Warm Love": Van Morrison
- "No Smoke without Fire": James Hunter
- "I've Got My Love to Keep Me Warm": Dean Martin
- "(Love Is Like a) Heat Wave": Martha and the Vandellas
- "In the Heat of the Night": Ray Charles
- "Shooting Star": Bob Dylan
- "Yellow": Coldplay

The rest of the world can rage away on Facebook and spend their mornings and evenings yelling at the television. We have chosen a different road, and no one else's anger and frustration can compel us to change direction. If you find yourself traveling on those same roads, we will probably end up seeing you at the campground.

Tip #6: Campfires Aren't Just for S'mores

Good conversation may feed the soul, but the body occasionally needs to indulge in a little snack, especially when relaxing around the campfire after an adventurous day. We enjoy cooking over an open fire, and we don't limit our campfire cravings to s'mores. Stephanie makes popcorn over the campfire, and we all love using pie irons to make grilled cheese sandwiches or mini pizzas. When the kids are particularly well behaved for long stretches of time, Stephanie might make her famous Dutch-oven monkey bread—and it's always a good time for a weenie roast followed by hot apples wrapped in foil.

Here's a pro tip for y'all: if the kids are going to dump those multicolored flame powders into the campfire, make sure that they wait to do so until after all of the over-the-fire cooking is done for the night. God only knows what kind of chemicals are used in those packets—they are most definitely not *organic*.

One night, I didn't realize that the boys had dumped a few packets into the campfire. I was halfway done roasting my hot dog before I noticed that the flames directly below it were purple and green. Maybe eating that hot dog would have given me superpowers, but I don't want that kind of additional responsibility. Being a father of three young boys is quite enough for me to contend with right now, thank you very much.

Tip #7: Dogs Are the Ultimate Campfire Accessory

Maggie was curled up around my legs that night when I threw the contaminated hot dog into the campfire, and she *was not happy with me*. Her full name is Maggie the Camping Dog, and she has absolutely changed our family for the better. We love camping with our dog, and we think you will too. Maggie loves a good campfire more than anyone else in the family. She picks her spot next to one of us when the campfire starts and heads back into the camper very reluctantly at the end of the night. Dogs really are the ultimate campfire accessory—they snuggle up next to you and help keep you warm, and they definitely keep you safe from any intruders, animal or otherwise. A dog curled up next to a crackling campfire just cranks the mojo up to a whole 'nother level, doesn't it?

Twelve Tips from Smokey Bear for Extinguishing a Campfire

1. Never cut whole trees or branches, dead or alive. Live materials won't burn, and dead standing trees—called "snags"—are often homes for birds and other wildlife.
2. Once you have a strong fire going, add larger pieces of dry wood to keep it burning steadily.
3. Don't burn dangerous things like aerosol cans, pressurized containers, glass, or aluminum cans. They could explode, shatter, and/or create harmful fumes or dust.
4. Keep your fire to a manageable size.
5. Make sure children and pets are supervised near the fire. Never leave your campfire unattended.
6. Allow the wood to burn completely to ash, if possible.
7. Pour lots of water on the fire. Drown *all* embers, not just the red ones. Pour until the hissing sound stops.
8. If you do not have water, stir dirt or sand into the embers with a shovel to bury the fire.
9. With your shovel, scrape any remaining sticks and logs to remove any embers. Make sure that no embers are exposed and still smoldering.
10. Continue adding water, dirt, or sand and stirring with a shovel until all material is cool.
11. Remember: if it's too hot to touch, it's too hot to leave.
12. Pack it in, pack it out. It is your responsibility to pack out everything that you packed in, including any trash.

(www.smokeybear.com)

Tip #8: Fully Extinguish the Campfire Each Night

Some nights I get so drowsy and relaxed around the campfire that it becomes tempting to not fully extinguish it before stumbling into bed. When I was a newbie camper, I sometimes committed this camping sin. I remember going to bed one night at a campground in Cape Cod without putting the fire all the way out. As I was drifting off to sleep, I heard foot-steps outside the RV, so I peeked out the window. A man was dousing my campfire, which had revved back up, with a bucket of water. He looked like the manager of the campground, but it was too dark to tell. I was totally embarrassed. Later that week, I found out that all of Cape Cod was on high alert for forest fires because it was very dry that summer.

From that point forward, I vowed to always fully extinguish my camp-fire with water before going to bed. It only takes an extra minute, and it can save lives and protect our campgrounds and most-cherished locations.

Tip #9: Morning Campfires Rock!

There's nothing better than a warm campfire under the stars, but a warm campfire on a chilly morning comes mighty close. When we camp in the cool fall months, we often light a fire to keep us warm while we are cooking breakfast nearby. The boys love to run around and play on those cool mornings, and they will often drop by the fire to warm up before heading back out into the woods for manhunt or hide-and-seek. If you light the campfire in the morning and you are camping with friends nearby, they will often wander over to warm up their hands and say hello. The campfire has a magnetic pull that appeals to our deepest human desires for warmth and connection. We truly hope that you find your way to the campground this season and pull up a chair around the original social network.

Five Warm Drinks for Chilly Nights around the Campfire

The Classic Hot Toddy

This isn't a new or unusual hot beverage, but it's a classic. And for good reason. Everyone has heard of a hot toddy, but so many people have never actually tried one. Now's your chance. They are simple and delicious. Plus, they warm you right up from the toes to the nose.

Ingredients

▷ ¾ cup water

▷ 1 shot whiskey

▷ 2 to 3 teaspoons honey, to taste

▷ Squeeze of lemon juice, to taste

Heat the water. Stir in the whiskey, honey, and lemon juice to taste. The key to making the perfect hot toddy is to adjust the amounts of whiskey, honey, and lemon to suit your own personal taste. I like to go stronger on the whiskey and lemon and lighter on the honey because I don't like my drinks overwhelmingly sweet.

You do you.

Warm Pumpkin Spice Rum Cocktail

Apparently the whole world is wild for pumpkin spice, so we had to include one pumpkin drink in our list of favorite hot drinks. If a pumpkin spice latte is your jam, but you are done caffeinating for the day, try out this treat. Some folks like to use the dairy-free pumpkin spice coconut milk from So Delicious, but you can use plain coconut milk too.

Ingredients

- 1 cup coconut milk
- 1 shot dark rum
- 1 shot vanilla vodka
- Pinch of cinnamon
- Pinch of pumpkin pie spice
- Pumpkin puree, to taste (optional)

Warm the first five ingredients together and enjoy! If you really, really like pumpkin, whisk in some pumpkin puree.

Hot S'mores Cocktail

This recipe is the most fun because the first step is to make your own "graham cracker liquor" in advance. Combine a liter of white rum, one cinnamon stick, and half a cup of honey. Let that sit for four days, shaking once a day. Now bring your graham cracker liquor to the campground and get ready for s'more time...

Ingredients

- 1 shot brandy
- 1 tablespoon graham cracker liquor
- 1 cup prepared hot chocolate
- Mini marshmallows, to taste

Pour the brandy and graham cracker liquor into a mug. Fill the mug with hot chocolate. Top with mini marshmallows (of course!). Let the little guys walk around with ooey-gooey fingers while you sip your sweet, non-sticky drink.

Mulled Wine

We feel like this classic hot beverage gets brushed aside as old fashioned and out of style. But it's really yummy and warming. It's basically the winter version of sangria, and sangria's hip, so...

The most important tip we can offer is to use a dry red wine. If you use something sweet, it will end up cloying and overbearing.

Ingredients

- 1 bottle dry red wine
- 4 cups apple cider
- 1/4 cup honey
- 2 cinnamon sticks
- 4 whole cloves
- 3 whole star anise
- Juice and zest of 1 orange
- Orange slices for garnish

Combine everything in a saucepan and bring to a boil. Reduce heat and simmer for 10 minutes. Some folks make this in a Crock-Pot and then just keep it warm for serving at tailgates and around the campfire.

Spiked Peppermint Hot Chocolate

You can make this as easy or as complicated as you wish. For the hot chocolate, keep it simple by using a mix packet, or heat a cup of milk and melt in delicious semisweet chocolate squares.

Ingredients

- ▷ 1 shot peppermint schnapps
- ▷ 1 cup prepared hot chocolate
- ▷ Whipped cream, to taste
- ▷ Crushed peppermint candies or mini chocolate chips, for garnish

Pour the peppermint schnapps into a mug. Fill the mug with hot chocolate. Top with whipped cream and garnish with crushed peppermint candies or mini chocolate chips. You can make a mocktail version of this by simply adding a drop of peppermint extract to the kiddies' hot chocolates!

CAMP-FOOD
Rules

STEPHANIE

When we first started camping with our eleven-month-old twin boys, I made two really big mistakes in the camp-food department. The first bad move I made was trying to replicate what I remembered from my family's camping trips when I was a child. I recalled my mother cooking up a storm in the weeks leading up to our trips. She would plan and prep for elaborate meals that she would then cook on a camp stove or over an open fire at the campground. One thing that particularly stands out in my memory is when she made homemade pie crust for campfire apple pies. I still remember helping her cut perfect circles of uncooked pie crust and then layering the discs with wax paper before stacking them in the cooler. That was a lot to live up to for a working mom of twin babies who just wanted to have a bit of fun on the weekends.

It honestly took me a couple of years to stop trying to re-create what I thought of as an authentic camp-food experience. I had to come to terms with the fact that I was not my mother, and I didn't even necessarily want to do everything the same way that she had. My mom never worked outside the home, and she was perfectly happy to spend a *lot* of her time preparing food. I, on the other hand, was a full-time educator who would often rather take a hike than bake a pie. I finally embraced the fact that it was absolutely possible to be a great mom and not produce Pinterest-worthy meals at the campground.

Now, the ironic part of this story is that over the years, as our babies have grown up and become less likely to eat dirt when left unattended, I've been able to have a lot more fun cooking at the campground. In fact, it's become an enjoyable family hobby, and we all have our favorite meals both to prepare and to eat. The real moral of this story is that camp food should be whatever works for your family at any given time in your life. And you shouldn't let pictures on social media tell you any differently.

The second mistake I made was not investing the time and money into stocking a great camp kitchen. I happen to be a bit frugal by nature and, after buying the pop-up camper, the last thing I wanted to do was spend money on gear. I convinced myself that I had enough old pots, pans, and dishes from college to get us by. I also listened to some bad advice from other campers and filled in the gaps at my local dollar store, purchasing a can opener, measuring cups, and other odds and ends.

Here's the thing about stocking a camp kitchen with old, cheap junk from your basement and bargain stores: it turns the challenging task of campground cooking into a nearly impossible burden. I burned the bottom of pots. I melted plastic spoons. I cut myself trying to chop onions with a dull knife. It took a little while for the lightbulb to turn on, but I finally realized that camp cooking was more fun and the food was a lot more delicious when I actually had the right tools for the job.

Don't get me wrong—you don't have to spend a lot of money stocking a camp kitchen. But you really should spend a little something if you're starting from scratch. There is a lot of high-quality and affordable cooking gear out there that's made to withstand the elements. I would have been better off with two well-made cast-iron pans than I was with my whole set of cheap pots from college.

I love food, and I love cooking. The challenge for me as a new camper was making camp food something to enjoy and not something that caused me stress and anxiety. Years later, after a lot of trial and error, campground meals are where some of our happiest family memories are made. Here are the camp-food rules I live by.

Camp-Food Commandments

Plan and Prep in Advance

Even if you plan on keeping things very simple and low-key, it's still wise to do some advance planning and preparation before heading to the camp-ground. I never realize how many things I take for granted until I try to prepare food anywhere but my home kitchen. So no matter what, I write out a menu and make a packing list of everything I need for each meal. I got religious about this rule after one too many trips where I didn't have the mayo to go with the tuna or the buns to go with the hot dogs.

If you have the time, chopping vegetables, mixing spice rubs, and mar-inating meats ahead of time will make cooking at the campground a breeze. But if you are too busy to do anything except throw all your ingredients in coolers or the RV refrigerator, don't fret. You'll be just as happy dicing garlic at a campground picnic table.

Take the Time to Create Fully Stocked Camp Kitchen

This rule applies whether you are tent camping, cabin camping, or RVing. One of the things that made our camping trips so complicated in the begin-ning was that I was packing so many things for every single trip. I'm not exaggerating when I say that I didn't have a dedicated can opener, potato peeler, or bottle opener for the pop-up. Sometimes I remembered every-thing. And sometimes I didn't. I'll never forget that special kind of emo-tion that rolls over you on a Friday night when you realize that you have a bottle of wine and nothing to open it with. Now we have a travel trailer, so I can keep all my kitchen supplies stocked in the cabinets and drawers at all times, but we still have an entirely separate set of plastic bins in the garage that contain our camp-kitchen supplies for tent and cabin camping.

One pro tip for you: it's better to have a few smaller kitchen bins than one huge bin. I once bought a giant plastic bin that technically fit everything we needed for our tent-camping kitchen setup. The size made it completely unwieldy to pack and unpack. Plus, I was constantly digging through everything searching for the item I wanted. That bin was quickly replaced by three smaller ones.

Take the Time to Create a Fully Stocked Camp Pantry

It's amazing how hard it is to remember all the "pantry" items that we need to cook at the campground. I can name so many things that I used to forget on a regular basis (taco seasoning, balsamic vinegar, baking powder, etc.) before I kept a fully stocked pantry bin. I don't like storing food in our RV while we aren't camping, but I do keep an airtight bin of food staples in our garage that can easily be packed without a second thought, whether we are RVing, cabin camping, or tent camping. If I'm getting low on salt, pepper, olive oil, or sugar, I just make a note in my phone so I remember to restock when we get home!

Plan a Mix of Familiar Foods and Special Camping Foods

Even the most adventurous kids often crave routine and familiarity when traveling. Food is such an easy way to bring the comforts of home to the campground. I make sure to mix in some special camping meals with favorites from our regular dinner rotation at home. That means one night we might have chicken and veggies cooked in tinfoil packets over the campfire, and the next night will be regular old tacos, a big hit in our house.

This goes for other meals as well. We used to do huge pancake breakfasts every morning at the campground. Now we know to mix those up with simple breakfasts like oatmeal, cereal, bagels, and smoothies. This way we have special camping meals that our boys really enjoy, but we keep it manageable for us as parents.

Have a Few Set Shopping Lists and Menus

If you love sitting down the week before a camping trip and making completely unique menus and shopping lists every time...more power to you! I did that for quite some time and often ended up feeling overwhelmed and stressed out. A few years ago, I sat down and made a few set menus and paired them up with grocery-shopping lists. I made three menu/grocery-list documents: one for regular weekend trips, one for long weekends, and one for weeklong vacations. It was completely transformative.

Now if I feel like I'm too busy to plan anything new, I just pull out one of my set menus and sometimes even order the groceries through an online delivery service. If I have the time to be creative, however, I just substitute out some regular menu items with a special meal. Knowing that I have a plan even when I don't have time to plan helps keep family camping trips easy and fun.

Find Your Own Camp-Cooking Style

It might take a little bit of trial and error to find the cooking style that fits your family at the campground. I am an enthusiastic home cook, and I really love making healthy, delicious meals at home. But when I tried to bring that same style of cooking to the campground, it didn't quite work out the way I had envisioned. The same thing kept happening over and over again. We would be out exploring all day, hiking, kayaking, and having a great time. When we came back to the campground, everyone would be famished. Unfortunately, I had often planned elaborate Dutch-oven meals that would take hours to prepare.

I ended up embracing slow-cooker meals and frozen casseroles in a way I never would have imagined. We began to make more dinners on the grill than over the campfire. Now I understand that we have different kinds of camping trips as a family, and I adjust my cooking style accordingly. If we are road-tripping, I keep it simple and fast because we are exploring an area and not necessarily hanging out at the campground. If we are spending a lazy weekend camping with friends, we bust out the Dutch oven and get creative.

See You *at the* Campground

Enjoy Local Food Culture while Traveling

One of the best things about camping versus staying in a hotel is being able to prepare your own meals. For us, the very worst part of a hotel vacation is the never-ending meals out in restaurants. However, we also love to enjoy the local food culture when visiting a new or favorite destination. We live for lobster rolls in Maine, chicken and waffles in South Carolina, tacos in Texas, and chowder in Oregon.

A little advance planning keeps our foodie adventures kid and budget friendly. We also try to eat out for lunch instead of dinner. The price tag is cheaper and the atmosphere is usually more casual. We look for farms and farm stands where we can buy (or pick!) local specialties and enjoy them back at our campsite. Plus, we always consult one of our favorite resources, *Roadfood* by Jane and Michael Stern. They have led us to the yummiest roadside dives all over the country.

Keep It Fun!

After a couple of years of camping, I noticed a reoccurring theme that led me to make a lot of changes to the way we cooked at the campground. I often got stressed out by planning the menu before a trip, so I decided to make the preparation a lot simpler. I sometimes became overwhelmed at the campground trying to make dinner with little kids underfoot, so I ditched elaborate camp-cooking methods and focused on fast, easy dinners. I also learned that the most important part of all was sitting down for a meal with my family. It didn't matter what was on our plates. We might have been eating peanut butter and jelly with sliced apples, but we were as happy as could be because we were together.

Easy Campfire Cooking with Kids

As soon as our boys were out of the dirt-eating stage, we started to enjoy some really simple meals that we could cook together over the campfire. Now, we weren't baking bread or making beef stew in a Dutch oven. We embraced the simple pleasures of a hot dog on a roasting fork, and soon that became one of our boys' favorite Friday night dinners at the campground. Sometimes we would get fancy and wrap canned biscuit dough around the hot dog for our campfire version of pigs in a blanket. The best part of this tradition was simply spending time together, making and eating food around the campfire, and reconnecting after a busy week.

Over the years, although we still continue to enjoy a good weenie roast, we've expanded our menu of meals that we cook together as a family over the campfire. Pie-iron and foil-packet dinners are both in regular rotation on our camping trips.

Pie Irons

Pie irons come in two versions, cast iron and cast aluminum, and are basically the panini press of campfire cooking. Years ago, we fell in love with the Toas-Tite brand of pie irons, which are cast aluminum. We like that they are lighter than the cast-iron ones and a bit easier to care for and keep clean. However, other people will swear by cast iron. Either way, we recommend having one per family member, so no one has to wait too long to make their dinner. If you are a garage-sale or thrift-store fan, keep your eye out for pie-iron bargains. These items often show up in secondhand stores, and most shoppers don't even know what they are.

When it comes to pie-iron dinners, you are only limited by your creativity. We will take any type of sandwich or wrap that we all like and put it into the pie iron. Here are some of our favorites.

PIE-IRON PIZZA

Ingredients:

- Two slices wheat bread
- Marinara or pizza sauce
- Shredded mozzarella
- Pepperoni (or any of your favorite pizza toppings)

Grease the pie iron with spray, oil, or butter. Place one slice of wheat bread on the pie iron. Spoon on the marinara sauce. Sprinkle the mozzarella. Add the pepperoni or any other toppings. Top with the second slice of wheat bread. Close the pie iron and toast over the campfire for about two minutes on each side.

PIE-IRON HAM SAMMIES

Ingredients:

- Two slices rye bread
- Deli-sliced provolone cheese
- Deli-sliced ham
- Honey mustard sauce (We make our own, but you can buy premade, if you wish.)

Grease the pie iron with spray, oil, or butter. Place one slice of rye bread on the pie iron. Spread the honey mustard sauce on the bread. Layer the cheese and ham on top. Place the second slice of rye bread on top of the sandwich. Close the pie iron and toast over the campfire for about three minutes on each side. (We find that you need some more toasting time if your cheese is in slices rather than shredded!)

PIE-IRON TURKEY REUBENS

Ingredients:

- Two slices pumpernickel bread
- Sliced Swiss cheese
- Deli-sliced turkey
- Sauerkraut
- Thousand Island dressing

Grease the pie iron with spray, oil, or butter. Place one slice of pumpernickel bread on the pie iron. Layer the cheese and turkey on the bread. Spoon the sauerkraut and Thousand Island dressing on top. Place the second slice of pumpernickel bread on top of the sandwich. Close the pie iron and toast over the campfire for about three minutes on each side. (We find that you need some more toasting time if your cheese is in slices rather than shredded!)

PIE-IRON TASTY TACOS

Ingredients:

- Two small flour tortillas
- Cooked leftover taco beef
- Rice
- Black beans
- Grated cheddar cheese
- Salsa
- Sour cream
- Guacamole

We double our taco Tuesday recipe at home and then use the leftovers for this yummy treat at the campground the following weekend! Grease the pie iron with spray, oil, or butter. Place one small flour tortilla on the pie iron. Spoon on the meat, rice, and beans. Layer the cheese and salsa on top. Place the second tortilla on top. Close the pie iron and toast over the campfire for about three minutes on each side. Serve with sour cream and/or guacamole on the side!

PIE-IRON DESSERT FOR DINNER

Ingredients:

- Two whole-grain waffles
- Nutella
- Strawberries or raspberries

Grease the pie iron with spray, oil, or butter. Place one waffle on the pie iron. Spread the Nutella on the waffle. Layer your fruit of choice on top of the Nutella. Place the second waffle on top. Close the pie iron and toast over the campfire for about two minutes on each side.

Foil Packets

Foil-packet dinners are basically our version of a buffet at the campground. These are especially popular right now, since we have two adventurous eaters and one very picky eater. Using heavy-duty tinfoil, we let the boys create their own foil packet by choosing from any of the uncooked meat and veggies that we lay out. Once they've put in their ingredients, we wrap the foil tight to create a seal and place the pouch into the hot campfire coals to cook. These are so ridiculously delicious for how simple they are to prepare. Plus, they are perfect for individuals with certain food restrictions or allergies. It's easy to tweak the ingredients of a foil packet without changing the whole meal.

Foil-packet dinners are almost, but not quite, mistake-proof. I've managed to learn these seven valuable lessons the hard way over the last few years.

1　Always use heavy-duty tinfoil. Believe me, I've tried to substitute the cheap stuff in a pinch and have been very sorry when the pouch broke open and dumped delicious food into the campfire ashes.

2　Use cooking spray on the inside of the foil packet before putting in your ingredients. Is there anything worse than bits of tinfoil stuck to your food?

3　Place the meat, if you are using any, at the bottom of the foil packet so it comes in contact with the coals and cooks thoroughly.

4　Don't include ingredients that will take too long to cook compared to the rest of the food. Potatoes, pasta, and rice should be cooked ahead of time and added in at the end.

5　Always include a nice, flavorful sauce or broth so that the ingredients can steam inside the foil packet.

6   Take your time creating a very tight fold across the top of the foil packet. If you just crunch it together, you probably won't get a good enough seal for the ingredients to steam inside.

7   Cook the foil packets over hot coals, *not* over flames. If you put your pouch directly over flames, you'll wind up with a burned, smoky mess of a meal.

------- **Beginner Cast-Iron Pots, Pans, and Accessories** -------

Want to start cooking with cast iron? Get started with this basic gear setup:

- ☐ 10 1/2-inch or 12-inch cast-iron skillet
- ☐ 3.2-quart cast-iron combo cooker from Lodge
- ☐ flaxseed oil for seasoning
- ☐ Lodge 10-inch scrub brush
- ☐ Lodge pan Scrapers, set of two
- ☐ silicone or leather handle holders
- ☐ outdoor cooking gloves

Dutch-Oven and Cast-Iron Cooking: Basics for Beginners

Is there a more iconic camping image than cooking in a Dutch oven over an open fire? A Dutch oven is a type of cast-iron pot that comes in a variety of sizes and can be used to make everything from stew to pizza to baked cobblers.

The most important thing to know about Dutch-oven cooking is that it does take more time and attention than most other forms of meal preparation. So if you are starting out your camping adventures with very young children, don't feel like you have to master the art of cooking over a campfire. It might be best to save this fun hobby for when your kids have a good understanding of campfire safety and can entertain themselves with books or bikes while you make the magic happen.

The second most important thing to know is that quality does matter. There are really cheap options that might seem tempting, but you will not be able to make great food without a good quality pot. We think the iconic Lodge cast-iron products are the best value, combining an affordable price point with reliable craftsmanship.

Our last beginner tip is to keep it simple until you've mastered the basics. Purchase a few high-quality workhorse pots, pans, and accessories as a starter kit and then practice with simple and delicious family favorites. I highly recommend starting out with more forgiving recipes like soup and stew before diving into baked goods, which require a bit more precision in terms of heat and timing.

Here are some of our family's favorite beginner Dutch oven recipes to get you started.

DUTCH-OVEN BREAKFAST SCRAMBLE

The great thing about this dish is that it can easily be adjusted to your family's personal tastes, and it is just about impossible to mess up.

Ingredients:

- Breakfast meat (sausage, bacon, or diced Canadian ham)
- Vegetables (we like green peppers, onions, mushrooms, and tomatoes)
- Eggs
- Grated cheese (cheddar, Swiss, or pepper jack)

Directions:

1. Start off by browning your favorite breakfast meat in a preheated, greased Dutch oven.
2. Add vegetables, if desired, and cook until tender.
3. Scramble however many eggs it takes to feed your hungry campers, and add the eggs to the meat and vegetable mixture.
4. Throw in a handful of grated cheese. Place the lid on the Dutch oven and cook until the cheese is melted and the eggs are set.

You can serve this with toast or potatoes. Our kids like it best served burrito-style, in soft tortillas with a dollop of sour cream and salsa.

Fantastic Cast-Iron Recipe Books

- *Lodge Cast Iron Nation: Great American Cooking from Coast to Coast*
- *Cook It in Cast Iron: Kitchen-Tested Recipes for the One Pan That Does It All*
- *The Lodge Cast Iron Cookbook: A Treasury of Timeless, Delicious Recipes*
- *The Cast Iron Skillet Cookbook: Recipes for the Best Pan in Your Kitchen*

DUTCH-OVEN PIZZA

A little prep work at home will make this one of the easiest—and most fun—campground dinners you will ever prepare. We do all of our vegetable chopping ahead of time and also bring along some frozen homemade meatballs...a favorite topping in our family.

Ingredients:

- Store-bought pizza dough
- 1 (14.5-ounce) jar pizza sauce
- Vegetable and meat toppings
- 2 cups mozzarella cheese

Directions:

1. Roll out the pizza dough so that it fits snugly in the bottom of a well-greased Dutch oven. We keep it simple and use store-bought dough, but if you are feeling fancy, go ahead and make your own.
2. Spread the pizza sauce on top of the dough.
3. Add any vegetable and meat toppings that you like.
4. Place the Dutch oven directly on the hot coals and close the lid. Many people like to place coals on the lid as well for more even cooking.
5. After about 15 minutes, open the lid and top the pizza with the mozzarella cheese. Cook for another 5 minutes or until the crust is brown and the cheese is bubbly.

DUTCH-OVEN MONKEY BREAD

Take a break from s'mores one night and make this for a campfire treat instead. The kids will love it. And let's face it...adults will too.

Ingredients:

- ½ cup brown sugar
- ½ cup sugar
- 3 tablespoons cinnamon
- 2 canisters refrigerated biscuit dough
- 1 stick butter, and chopped walnuts (optional)

Directions:

1. Line the Dutch oven with tinfoil. (This step is very important if you don't want to tear your hair out during cleanup.) Mix the brown sugar, sugar, and cinnamon in a large ziplock bag.

2. Open the canisters of biscuit dough. Rip each biscuit into quarters and drop them into the cinnamon-sugar mixture. Shake well to coat. Place the biscuit pieces in the Dutch oven.

3. Melt the butter and drizzle it over the biscuits. Top with chopped walnuts, if desired.

4. Place the Dutch oven over hot coals, put on the lid, and cover the top with coals to evenly distribute the heat. Cook for about 30 to 40 minutes, rotating the pot and refreshing the coals halfway through.

The monkey bread is done when the dough is puffy and slightly browned. This dessert will disappear fast...and become a top-requested menu item for future camping trips!

Grills, Griddles, and Camp Stoves

Cooking outside is such a treat for us whether we are RVing, cabin camping, or tent camping. Even though we have a full kitchen in our family RV, we still cook and eat outside as much as possible. Many RVs (ours included) come with a grill. These freebie grills are sometimes jokingly called RVQs, and let me tell you, they are almost always complete junk! I struggled to cook on ours for about two years before finally throwing in the towel and buying a real grill.

Creating the perfect outdoor kitchen setup is worth the investment for many campers. Making and eating meals outside together as a family has been one of the most rewarding parts of our camping life. The good news is that there are a lot of very affordable, high-quality grills, griddles, and camp stoves available in big-box stores and online that are perfect for camp kitchens. The tricky part is narrowing down your options to the ones that will suit your needs the best.

CAMP STOVES

Before running out and adding that classic two-burner propane camp stove to your collection, ask yourself if you really need it. If you are tent camping, this is probably a must-have item. A camp stove will be a daily campground workhorse from the time you percolate your coffee in the morning to the time you heat up a can of baked beans for a side at dinner. You might also want to purchase a cast-iron griddle that sits over both burners and can cook bacon, eggs, pancakes, and burgers. However, if you are RVing or cabin camping, a camp stove might end up being a redundant piece of gear. Almost all RVs, even pop-up campers, come with a propane cooktop, and most cabins have a cooktop as well.

Remember those old, green Coleman camp stoves from your childhood Scouting adventures? They are still being manufactured and sold today... and they are still available in that classic green color, although you can also get a more modern black or gray finish. You can buy a classic Coleman propane stove along with a propane cylinder for about $50 and be ready to start cooking at the campground.

GRILLS

Picking out the perfect grill is a bit trickier, because there are so many options, and your cooking and travel style will determine which works best for you.

Charcoal

Some folks swear by charcoal, and we love grilling over charcoal at home. But at the campground, we are usually looking for a quicker, simpler grilling experience. For example, we often use our grill to heat up premade breakfast burritos in the morning. The last thing we want to do is light charcoal briquettes just to heat up a quick breakfast. We will also do quick hamburger and hot dog lunches during the day on our grill, so charcoal is a little fussy for the way we camp. If you love cooking with charcoal and want to do so at the campground, we recommend the Weber Jumbo Joe. It gets rave reviews from charcoal fans.

Propane

We have used and loved our Weber Q 1200 for years now, and it is one of our favorite pieces of camp gear ever. It's compact enough to easily fit in the storage bin of the RV or in the back of the truck when we are cabin or tent camping, but it's also big enough to cook steaks, chicken, or hamburgers for our entire family of five. If we have the camper, we can use the quick connect to tap right into our RV's propane supply. Otherwise, we just use the small propane canisters that we always keep stocked with our camping supplies. If you need more grilling space, the Weber Q 2200 is bigger but still very portable. Accessories like the grill stand and cover make this the perfect camping grill, in our opinion.

GRIDDLES

Recently, griddles have exploded in popularity among camping enthusiasts. The well-known company Camp Chef has been making outdoor griddles for years, but the price point, size, and weight kept this a relatively niche product for serious camp-cooking enthusiasts. Then an upstart company named Blackstone exploded onto the scene with more affordable and more portable seventeen-inch and twenty-two-inch propane griddles. Campers went wild.

At first, we thought this was just a passing fad. Then we bought our own Blackstone, and it became the single most-used piece of equipment in our camp kitchen. Why? Because it's incredibly versatile and cooks like a dream. We still love our Weber grill. But when we have to pick just one piece of outdoor cooking gear to bring on a trip, the twenty-two-inch Blackstone wins every time. We can cook all the items we would normally make on a grill, like hamburgers and steaks. Plus, we can cook everything else like pancakes, bacon, and scrambled eggs.

¤

The best camp-kitchen setup is the one that truly reflects how you want to cook and eat with your family at the campground. Are you looking to spend more time on the hiking trails than behind the camp stove? Keep it simple and easy and stress-free. Is your idea of happiness picking apples and then making homemade apple crisp back at the campground? Then get that Dutch oven fired up and ready. Just remember to keep your gear and your menus in line with your family's personal camping goals, and not with the goals of some stranger on Pinterest.

Pantry Checklist

Liquids

- ☐ oils (vegetable, olive)
- ☐ vinegars (red wine, balsamic)
- ☐ soy sauce
- ☐ nonstick cooking spray
- ☐ barbecue sauce
- ☐ hot sauce
- ☐ vanilla
- ☐ honey

Cans and Jars

- ☐ spaghetti sauce
- ☐ salsa
- ☐ beans
- ☐ tuna
- ☐ peanut butter
- ☐ jelly
- ☐ soup
- ☐ chicken broth

Dry Goods

- ☐ pasta
- ☐ rice
- ☐ corn-bread mix
- ☐ cereal
- ☐ oatmeal
- ☐ popcorn
- ☐ crackers
- ☐ granola bars
- ☐ sugar
- ☐ breakfast bars
- ☐ marshmallows
- ☐ graham crackers
- ☐ Hershey chocolate bars

Spices and Seasonings

- ☐ salt
- ☐ pepper
- ☐ taco seasoning
- ☐ seasoned salt
- ☐ garlic powder
- ☐ French onion mix
- ☐ Italian dressing mix
- ☐ favorite seasoning mixes

C amping is supposed to be relaxing and fun, right? Well for us, and for most camping enthusiasts, it usually is. Over the years, our family has stayed at hundreds of campgrounds, met countless new friends, and made amazing family memories.

We tell everyone we know that campers are such a friendly and polite group of people, and for the most part, it's true. However, there are always exceptions to the rule. Every once in a while, a camper doesn't follow the traditional guidelines for campground etiquette, and a peaceful camping retreat turns into a stressful experience you'd rather forget.

The golden rule works well for a lot of situations in life, but not necessarily for campground etiquette. Campers are a diverse group of people with different camping styles and preferences, so it's important to understand the basic guidelines that apply at all campgrounds, whether public or private, rustic or resort-style.

Now, before diving into the ins and outs of etiquette, it's worth remembering that if we want campgrounds to be well-mannered communities, then we should start by making sure that we are well mannered ourselves. Here are our three personal guidelines for ensuring positive campground experiences:

1. **Expect good things.** We go into every new campground wearing our rose-colored glasses. Attitude goes a long way toward creating happy campers. If you search for the negative, you will probably find it.

2. **Let the little things go.** Don't allow little annoyances to ruin your entire stay. If your temporary next-door neighbor wakes you before quiet hours are over, try not to stew about it. Pop in some earplugs and go back to bed.

3. **Talk to campground management about any issues.** If someone or something is impacting the quality of your camping experience, ask the right people to help solve the problem. This will often yield better results than individual confrontations or social media rants.

Now on to the nitty-gritty. If you're a newbie, consider this your primer on campground etiquette. If you're a seasoned camper, think of it as a refresher course.

Campground Etiquette Basics

Shared Spaces and Common Ground

Campgrounds take a lot of strangers and put them into a relatively small amount of space, so it's very important for everyone to be on their best behavior. Here are six guidelines to observe while enjoying the communal areas of the campground:

1 **Follow the rules of the campground you choose to visit.** When you make a reservation at a particular campground, you are agreeing to abide by their rules during the entirety of your stay. Some places have very specific policies about golf carts, campfires, and curfews. If you don't like the rules, stay somewhere else.

2 **Drive slowly and obey traffic directions.** We believe that there is never a reason to drive over five miles an hour in a campground. People are walking dogs, riding bikes, and playing catch. Nothing gets campers on edge more than folks who treat campground roads like speedways. In addition, always obey one-way signs, whether they make sense to you or not. No one wants to end up in a game of chicken with a Class A motorhome on a single-lane road.

Reminders for Young Children

Many kids don't realize when they are breaking unwritten rules of the campground. Remind your little ones to take the following steps.

- Stay on established roads and paths.
- Abide by rules of the road on bikes, scooters, and skateboards.
- Take turns on playground equipment and in other recreational areas.

3 **Respect shared spaces and monitor children at all times.**
Playgrounds and pools can be hot spots for controversy at the campground. Don't reserve tables or chairs for the entire day if you are
not physically present at the pool, and if you're camping with a large
group, make sure your cannonball contest isn't keeping others from
enjoying a nice swim.

No matter how safe a campground is, don't allow your kids to roam
unattended. Other adults get frustrated when there are issues at the
playground or the jumping pillow and no parent can be found.

4 **Discard all garbage and recycling in the proper containers.** Every
campground has different garbage and recycling policies, so make sure
you are properly informed upon check-in. Some campgrounds offer
garbage pickup at the campsite, but leaving food scraps out overnight
can lead to undesirable wildlife encounters. We keep any bags of garbage closed up tight in the back of our truck until we are able to dispose
of them properly.

5 **Respect shared bathhouses by leaving them clean for the next
camper.** Wash dishes in sinks designated for that purpose and not in
the bathroom sinks. Bathhouse garbage cans are intended for small
pieces of trash and not for bags of garbage from your site. We also
recommend making note of the times when the bathhouses are closed
for cleaning, so that you don't get caught in an uncomfortable situation!
You might also consider showering during off-hours when the bathhouses are less busy and (probably) cleaner. Always bring shower shoes!

6 **Thank camp workers and managers for exceptional service, and
leave positive reviews for great campgrounds.** Remember how you
were taught when you were growing up to always say please and
thank you? Bring those best manners to the campground. We always

take note when we receive great customer service and look to pass compliments on to management. Leaving positive reviews also helps other campers find locations where they can expect great service and a friendly atmosphere.

Tending to Your Own Plot of Land

Even though you may only be staying for a short time, it's important to be a good neighbor at the campground. Respect the fact that people are camping nearby and that other folks will be using the campsite once you're gone.

1 **Observe campsite boundaries.** One of the most common complaints on camping forums and social media is about people who cut through campsites. Never use a campsite as a shortcut, and stay on clearly marked paths whenever you're walking around the campground. Make sure to pass this wisdom on to your children as well.

--------------- **Most Unpopular Transgressions** ---------------
- cutting through another camper's site
- leaving a barking dog unattended at the campsite
- being noisy during campground quiet hours

2 **Be conscious of noise.** Def Leppard might be your jam at the campground, but not everybody shares your taste in music. With the abundance of outdoor speakers and televisions on new RVs, it's important to remember that noise shouldn't travel far beyond your own slice of real estate. Test the volume by taking a walk to a neighboring site. If you can still hear Steely Dan, it's time to turn it down a few notches. In addition, quiet hours are observed religiously at many campgrounds. Know the policy where you are camping and keep it down during that time.

3 **Be a responsible dog owner.** We love traveling with our dog, but irresponsible pet owners are another one of the most common campground-etiquette complaints out there on the interwebs. Always keep dogs on a six-foot leash when walking and make sure they are properly restrained on the campsite at all times via a tether or expandable pen. Carry bags (or use ones provided by the campground) to dispose of pet waste properly.

Perhaps most importantly, no one (not even the most ardent dog lover) appreciates incessant barking. If your pup yaps nonstop at the campground, you might consider leaving him or her with a sitter during your camping trips.

4 **Enjoy your campfire safely.** When it comes to the campfire, take a cue from the Boy Scouts and put safety first. Only build fires in approved rings or pits and never leave a campfire unattended. Put it out completely with water before retiring for the night. Other no-no's? Never burn trash or place glass in a campground firepit. That just leaves a big mess for the next campsite resident.

5 **Turn off all exterior lights at night.** As much as you love those cool
LED awning lights on your new RV, your neighbor in the pop-up
camper or tent might not appreciate them so much. A good rule of
thumb is to treat quiet hours as dark hours too. Double-check to make
sure all your exterior lights are turned off before turning in for the night.

6 **Leave the campsite just as you found it.** Remember that the campsite
is just on loan to you for a short while, so it's important not to make any
permanent changes. Don't move boundary stones or fire rings, and if
you move the picnic table, return it to where it was before you leave.

Never, ever, ever cut down any trees or branches, and don't put nails in
trees for clotheslines or hammocks. Before departing, do a quick sweep
of the site to check for any personal items or debris.

Making Friends Instead of Enemies

Most of us spend a lot of time behind screens these days, interacting with people on social media more than in person. Dust off your social skills at the campground, and look for these three opportunities to be friendly just like in the neighborhoods of old.

1 **Let people focus when parking, hitching, and unhitching their RVs.** Talking to campers while they are trying to back in their trailer or hitch up to leave is not just distracting—it can be downright dangerous. Give people their space, even if you think you could get them into that difficult site in a flash. Oh, and try not to stare...we were all rookies once.

2 **Help rookies if they ask.** We'll never forget the time when three seasoned campers helped us get our propane heater lit on a cold fall night. They saved us from disaster, and we have heard many similar stories over the years. Passing on expertise is a truly wonderful tradition in RV culture.

3 **Pay it forward.** Our day has been brightened many times by the thoughtfulness of other folks at the campground, and we appreciate the opportunity to pay it forward when we travel. Leaving behind unused firewood for the next camper is a nice gesture, or you can walk it over to your neighbor at the next site before you depart. We have also loaned folks an extra hose to reach their hookups and given neighbors a fuse when they had one blow. It's often these little things that make the campground experience such a special thing.

⊐

We believe that camping etiquette is not just about following a list of rules. It's really about creating a thoughtful, friendly, and polite environment where everyone realizes that their actions impact other people. Time at the campground is precious—we go there to relax, have fun, and enjoy the company of our family and friends. Let's make sure not to ruin that for anyone else!

W e started camping when our first two kids were eleven months old because of our dreams for the future. I can honestly say that it wasn't because we had some parenting vision that involved raising our boys in the woods. We loved travel. We loved road trips. And we wanted to keep having fun in spite of the drastic changes that happened as soon as our twin babies entered the picture. In hindsight, though, I feel so incredibly lucky that we bought that pop-up camper. I didn't realize it at the time, but it was exactly the right decision to help us raise our kids according to values that have become very important to us as parents.

Anyone who has kids knows that the early years can be like a fog. You emerge from those baby years feeling a bit confused and disoriented, wondering what just happened. Well, as we left that baby stage behind us, we started to realize that our efforts were truly paying off. Even though it wasn't entirely by design, we had managed to create a life that was encouraging our boys to grow in many areas that were important to us, like patience, creativity, and curiosity.

At the time, we felt that many of these traits were limited to our actual camping experiences. I would see the boys engage in imaginative play at the campsite in ways that wouldn't necessarily translate to our backyard.

But over the years, I have been amazed to watch these traits translate to every area of their life, including academics and organized sports.

So, yes, I am thankful that I have taken my children to Cadillac Mountain in Acadia National Park, where the sun first strikes the eastern shore of the United States each morning. And I'm also grateful that they have stood next to some of the largest redwood trees in the world on California's coast. But I am more grateful that we stumbled into this whole camping lifestyle when they were itty-bitty babies—their lives will be forever better because of it.

The Many Gifts of Camping

I can see now that we have been giving our children the gifts of camping, and I look forward to watching as they benefit from them for years to come.

The Gift of Flexibility

I can admit that when I was a new parent, I was completely addicted to structure and routine. I don't think that was a bad thing. I firmly believe that it helped us avoid major breakdowns at key points in our journey. In fact, our commitment to routine even while traveling probably made our trips much more enjoyable, even when the boys were babies. We would keep the same bedtime, naptime, and meal habits. That gave the boys a sense of familiarity and kept them from being overwhelmed by all the unknown factors that come along with travel.

Nevertheless, we were constantly introducing them to new environments. On one of our earliest family camping trips, we stayed at four different campgrounds over the course of sixteen days. They had many familiar surroundings to help them feel secure (we actually traveled with their mini cribs in the pop-up camper...crazy, we know), but they had to adapt their expectations for each new place. Some of the campgrounds had pools and playgrounds, and some didn't. Over the years, we have watched them become masters at getting the lay of the land in a new location. They don't expect every place to be the same. They don't need a pool to have fun. Camping has taught them how to find the best things about any new environment and embrace the fun, whether we are in the mountains or a lake or a beachside resort.

I remember the time we traveled from a Jellystone campground in Sioux Falls, South Dakota, to Cedar Pass Campground in Badlands National Park. Our kids went from swimming in a heated pool to scrambling up clay and volcanic rock formations in the span of twenty-four hours and didn't even blink. I love that they know how to have a blast in a remarkable range of environments.

The Gift of Sociability

Many people talk about how the American neighborhood has changed over the last few decades, and we personally found that to be true as young parents. Our friends and family were scattered across different cities and states, and we barely knew the people who lived on our block.

When we started camping, we found that a lot of those traditional social interactions were alive and well at the campground. Folks sat out in their camp chairs waving to complete strangers who were walking by. It wasn't unusual to start up a conversation with a couple and wind up enjoying a potluck dinner together the next night. Camping introduced us to a culture where people are open to meeting new folks and starting new friendships. In fact, we now camp throughout the year with at least ten families that we met at various campgrounds.

This has been great for us, but more importantly, we've realized that it's had a profound impact on our kids. Our boys will make new friends at a campground within hours of us pulling in. They have no problem striking up a conversation with some kids at the playground. I've seen them independently introduce themselves and ask where the other kids are from. They know how to organize a pickup game of tag in a split second.

A couple of years ago, these experiences started having a positive effect on our neighborhood at home. I had gotten sucked into the playdate culture, organizing social interactions for my kids throughout their childhood. But they had reached the age where I wanted them to develop some social independence. I told the boys that I was done being their social secretary. If they wanted to play, they were going to have to go to their friends' houses, knock on the door, and ask if little Johnny could play.

At first they resisted, but soon enough they mustered the courage to walk a couple of houses down to see if their friends could play. Two years later, I cannot believe the impact that this has had on our neighborhood. I regularly have twelve or more kids playing in my backyard after school or riding bikes together around our loop of houses. They play manhunt across each other's yards and race scooters down the hill.

Max and Theo tell me that their friends at school, who are from the same town, think it's crazy that all the kids in our neighborhood knock on each other's doors every day after school and find out who can play. Apparently, they all think that we live in a super-fun part of town. I believe in my heart of hearts that we brought the campground back to our little slice of suburbia and, in a way, transformed our kids' childhood experience.

The Gift of Imaginative Play

We know that unscheduled, creative playtime is at risk for our kids. As much as we try to resist that, we get sucked into the busyness just like most other families out there do. When we are at home, our boys are constantly asking us what the next exciting event is. Even when we attempt to have lazy, laid-back Saturdays, the kids are asking for the schedule of activities by midmorning.

Camping puts us in a different environment and helps our children shift modes. They intuitively head into the woods and find sticks for sword fights. They swing each other in the hammock. They build sand castles when we are beach camping and try to catch crayfish when we are near a stream. Sticks, rocks, pickup games with kids at the campground. Even when there is a jumping pillow at the campground, they'll have seat-drop contests or play Mother May I with other kids.

Campsites with interesting natural features tend to really bring out our kids' creativity. I'll never forget one campsite in the White Mountains of New Hampshire. There was a giant rock at the side of our site, and our boys did nothing but play on that rock for four days straight. From that moment on, I understood how camping could inspire my boys to be more creative people.

The Gift of Physical Activity

Jeremy and I are naturally active people. Before the boys were born, we were never the type to be bored on a day off from work. Between surfing, yoga, gardening, biking, and other hobbies, we kept ourselves busy. When kids came along, getting out of the house became more complicated, and we noticed that our activity level went way down. Even now that they are older, we still struggle to spend as much time outside as we should. Going for a walk on our local boardwalk sometimes feels like more work than it's worth.

There is no doubt that we have a more active lifestyle when we are camping and traveling. The boys wake up in the morning and are on their bikes before breakfast is even ready. I've noticed that I walk the dog more when we are camping, since it's so easy to just stroll around the campground. We're more likely to look for nearby hiking spots or find a beautiful lake to launch the kayaks. The best part of this is that by the end of the day, the kids are completely worn out and fall asleep before their heads hit the pillow.

The Gift of Patience

I didn't grow up fishing, so when we started camping, it was not part of our usual routine. But campgrounds often have small catch-and-release ponds, so as the kids got older, they would regularly ask to fish. I'll never forget the first time I watched my three-year-old sit for almost an hour, trying to catch a little sunfish. This was a kid who never stopped moving, yet he was willing to wait quietly for a fish to find his bait.

The same thing happens on long car rides or challenging hikes. My boys are normally balls of energy who bounce from one thing to the next. So many parts of our camping life encourage them to wait patiently for the payoff.

The Gift of Curiosity

As someone who loves learning new things, I've always wanted my kids to be curious people. I wanted them to know that there is a big, beautiful world outside and it's worth exploring. I believe our camping trips helped establish that same curiosity in my children from a very young age. They know that the world outside of their own home is diverse. They know that different places will offer different types of adventures. I love that they are always excited to discover something new on our upcoming camping trips.

We've heard this feedback from teachers over and over again throughout the years. The boys' teachers always seem shocked by how diverse their knowledge is and how interested they are in thematic learning. I'm confident that's a direct result of our teaching them about the Civil War while touring Charleston or about the lobster industry on a boat in Maine.

The Gift of a Love for Nature

A little while ago, we were driving along the Badlands Loop State Scenic Byway, and we pulled the truck over to check out the prairie dog town. My boys were shocked and scandalized to find another family feeding pretzels to the animals. They went on and on about it for days: "Didn't they know it's wrong to do that? Don't they realize that it harms the prairie dogs?"

Their regular exposure to a wealth of nature and wildlife at state and national parks over the last decade has given the boys such a deep appreciation for the world around them. We never could have taught those same lessons from books or other media. The kids don't just know the rules of the Leave No Trace philosophy—they also understand the purpose behind it. They know how overfishing affected the ocean waters of New England and how the natural world recovered from the eruption of Mount St. Helens. I'm so grateful that my kids are in awe of nature.

The Gift of a Family Narrative

We had a lot of adventures when the boys were very young that we assumed they would never remember. But that wasn't the point to begin with. First of all, we wanted to have fun ourselves. Plus, we figured that we were training them up as our little adventure buddies for the future.

Well, it's shocking to us how much our kids actually do remember about our adventures. Apparently, a lot of these exciting moments have stuck with them. Of course, we are always retelling the highlights of trips again and again throughout the years, but it's also become a part of their identity. They think of themselves as explorers and travelers. They expect us to take them to epic destinations. And we are happy to deliver on that expectation year after year.

Developing Independence: Kids and Campground Safety

When deciding how we wanted to raise our kids, it initially felt like we had two options to pick from: free-range parenting or helicopter parenting. Neither style worked for us personally, and we knew we had to find a middle ground. Both of us wanted to raise our children to be independent and capable adults, but we certainly weren't willing to teach them life skills by letting them fend for themselves.

What Do Teens Really Think?

Ninety-six percent of teens say they appreciate that the adults in their lives are more relaxed while camping.

(KOA, 2018 North American Camping Report)

The campground became an amazing backdrop for us to give our boys guided independence as they grew and moved through different stages of childhood. We could allow them to ride their bikes around a loop with limited traffic danger. We could let them try their hand at purchasing ice cream at the camp store while we waited outside. We could watch them interact with other kids at the playground from our campsite across the way. Over the years, we have embraced the campground as a safe, somewhat contained place for us to develop our children's independence. They've been able to take those lessons and apply them to real-world situations at home.

There is no set of rules out there for how much freedom and independence your child can safely handle at any given age. I think most parents struggle with knowing exactly when their kids are ready for more responsibility. My background as an educator, including all of my courses on childhood development, has given me a bit more confidence in this area that has paid off in spades as I've let go and allowed my kids to try new things. So here are some general strategies and guidelines that we use when determining how far out of the nest our little birdies are ready to fly.

Pre-K Kids

If you want to raise a responsible, independent child, this is the time to start the hard work. Think about all the skills that it would take for a child to be safe without adult supervision, and begin training them very early on. Following are a few examples from our personal experience.

⇢ *Car and bicycle awareness:* We had our boys stop at the edge of the road and wave to cars that were driving by.

⇢ *Campsite awareness:* We always had our boys memorize our site number, so that they could get help if they got lost or separated.

⇢ *Basic stranger training:* Give specific guidance about which adults to seek out in case of trouble (campground employees, mothers with children). Talk about the difference between neighborly questions and tricky questions from other adults.

⇢ *Role-play scenarios:* I consistently ask my boys what they would do in certain circumstances. We talk about getting hurt, getting lost, other kids misbehaving, etc.

If you do these things for years, your children will be so much more prepared when they finally get old enough for some real independence at the campground and at home.

Elementary School Kids

For a few years, my boys would ask me how old they had to be before I finally let them walk home from the bus stop by themselves. I would always answer that there was no set age, but there *was* a level of responsibility. They hated that answer, but it's true.

There's no single age when kids are all of a sudden capable of going to the playground or the camp store by themselves. But as an elementary school teacher, I can tell you that many districts allow kids to independently ride their bikes and walk to and from school in third or fourth grade. That was a helpful guideline for us to use as parents.

However, before your kids are in middle school, you should be giving them tons of smaller opportunities to practice being independent. Here are a few things you can do at the campground:

- → Reserve a campsite just a few sites down from the playground, so your kids can play "by themselves," but you can watch them carefully from afar.

- → Let them ride in bicycle loops that you have preapproved.

- → Let them go into the camp store to buy something while you stay outside.

- → Have them lead you back to your campsite, so you can get a sense of their navigation abilities.

- → Let them go into the arcade by themselves while you wait outside.

When our nine-year-olds finally showed enough maturity to go play at the gaga ball pit by themselves, our favorite safety device was a set of walkie-talkies that helped us stay in constant contact with them. It gave them a way to contact us immediately, plus it calmed our nerves.

Preteens and Teenagers

Once your kids enter into those double digits, the honest truth is that it's not really about them. You have to be sure that your teens are mature enough not to be a danger to the younger kids who are also at the campground. One of the biggest campground-etiquette complaints we hear is from parents of younger kids. They hate it when groups of older kids take over jumping pillows, playgrounds, or pools and act in a way that makes it unsafe for the little ones.

If you're going to let your older kids enjoy the campground amenities and facilities independently, you have to do some legwork in advance. Talk very specifically about bicycle safety and watching out for younger children. Make sure that they are driving the golf cart in a safe way. And remind them *every single time* you arrive at a new campground to never, ever get into another person's car or enter another person's RV. Ever.

What's in It for the Parents?

We love our kids, but sometimes we really feel like they are totally taking over our lives. And of course, we are parenting during a particularly child-centered time in our culture. There are times when Jeremy and I realize that we have barely taken the time to connect with each other, much less given ourselves any individual care or attention.

That's not good for us, and it's certainly not good for our kids in the long run either. Investing in our marriage and making sure that our relationship was alive and well was one of the reasons we got our pop-up camper in the first place. We always wanted to have actual, real-life fun together as a couple. So the question is, has our road-trip and camping lifestyle contributed to this?

Absolutely. We spend a lot of time beating ourselves up for our missteps and failures as parents, but we believe that this wild and wacky camping lifestyle was a big, huge win for our marriage and for both of us as individuals. Looking back, here are the gifts that these family camping trips have given to us.

Top Five Reported Benefits of Camping

1. Reduces my stress from everyday life
2. Allows me to spend more time with family
3. Increases my emotional well-being
4. Makes me a healthier person
5. Improves my relationships with friends and family

(KOA, 2018 North American Camping Report)

The Gift of a Family Travel Template

When we begin to imagine our next big family adventure, we don't have to reinvent the wheel. Once we've decided on the destination, all the other pieces fall into place, thanks to our experience with planning camping trips. We are constantly having new, amazing experiences, but in a way, our travel style is a rinse-and-repeat formula. This makes all the difference for our stress levels as busy parents.

The Gift of Living in the Moment

When we are at home, both Jeremy and I are never without a physical or mental checklist for chores, errands, and activities. We often have a divide-and-conquer mentality, even on the weekends when we should be finding time to spend together. Sometimes we feel as if we are managing our life, instead of enjoying it. Our camping trips press the pause button on this hamster wheel. We feel it the second we pull into a campsite and unhitch. We both take a deep breath and focus on relaxing instead of doing. Every day at the campground starts with the question of what we want to enjoy, instead of what we need to accomplish.

The Gift of Appreciation for Our Own Backyard

It's easy to become a bit jaded about your own state or even your own country. Before we bought our pop-up, most of my dream vacations involved locations on other continents. RVing opened our eyes to the beauty and adventure that was in our own backyard. It's hard to believe that we didn't visit places like the Great Smokies or Shenandoah National Park until we camped there. Although we still look forward to exploring Iceland and Italy, right now we are content with some regional treasures that are much closer to home.

The Gift of Hobbies

Before I had kids, I enjoyed so many different hobbies, from gardening to yoga to baking. After having babies, those small pleasures seemed to drop off the radar one by one. Jeremy and I both believe that it's important for us to feed our own passions, but it's also so easy to get lost in the kids' interests and activities. Camping has been such an amazing opportunity to continue to grow and explore new hobbies even as adults and parents. Since we started RVing, we've added hiking, kayaking, biking, and paddle-boarding to our hobby list. Jeremy has learned how to cook in the great outdoors over the last couple of years, and I picked up the ukulele for the first time in decades.

The Gift of Simplicity and Minimalism

When we return from a two-week RV trip, I usually experience a sense of shock walking into our sticks-and-bricks home. It's an adjustment to realize just how much stuff we have and how much of it we don't even use. Our camping trips are a continual reminder that the less stuff we have, the more fun we usually have. It takes us maybe twenty minutes to clean up the RV if it's gotten messy. Our days at the campground aren't filled with laundry and tidying. The camping lifestyle continually reminds us to keep it simple at our everyday home as well.

The Gift of Communication, Teamwork, and Problem-Solving

Jeremy and I aren't one of those couples who never fight. We both have opinions about everything and are often convinced that the other person's opinions are wrong. Our camping and travel lifestyle demands that we work together and figure out our disagreements instead of retreating to separate rooms of the house. We work together as we plan trips, pack for adventures, drive to destinations, and set up the camper. It would probably be easier to be more independent of each other at home, but I'm grateful that our RVing lifestyle has encouraged us to work on our communication and teamwork skills over the years.

⋈

When we look at ourselves, our kids, and our marriage, it's truly overwhelming how much our lives have been impacted by our decision to buy that pop-up camper when the twins were eleven months old. Not every single moment of every single camping trip has been magical, but boy have they all been a blessing for our family.

CHAPTER

Fourteen

CAMPING *with*
FAMILY
and **FRIENDS**

JEREMY

During that same fateful spring when we bought our first RV, Stephanie's coworker Ashley and her husband Joe also bought their first RV. Soon after, we were planning camping trips with them. They also had two young, adventurous kids, Izzy and Morgan. We took weekend camping trips with them that spring and eventually started planning weeklong family vacations with them during the summer months. We made amazing memories during those shared trips to Acadia National Park, Cape Hatteras, the Finger Lakes, and Great Smoky Mountains National Park. They are some my favorite camping memories so far.

Max and Theo loved waking up each morning, dashing out of the RV, and finding their friends waiting for them at the next site. Stephanie and I loved putting the kids to bed and hanging out with friends around the campfire each night—and we all loved watching our kids gain strength and confidence together at the campground.

When I flip through old family photos and see us all together at the top of a mountain in Maine or tubing down a river in Tennessee, I always want to call Joe up and plan another RV trip. We helped watch each other's kids and gave each other little breaks from the constant responsibilities of parenting. We also cooked meals for each other and took turns cleaning up.

Looking back on those camping trips, it becomes clear to me that there are many advantages to camping together with family and friends and very few downsides. If you do it right.

Like so many other things in life (at least in our book) doing it right means planning ahead and opening up clear channels of communication. Our trips with Ashley and Joe went very smoothly because we really shared a similar camping style and similar taste in campgrounds. But when it came to camping with other friends and family, it did not always go so smoothly. Here's a case in point.

During our first summer of RV ownership, we planned a multi-family beach-camping trip to the KOA campground in Cape Hatteras with Stephanie's parents and her sisters. Stephanie and I picked the location, the campground, and the sites—then just passed the information on to her parents so they could make reservations. They didn't ask many questions about the campground, and we didn't provide them with many details. We loved beach camping and they loved beach camping, so we thought everyone would have a great time together! And we did. Kinda, sorta...

But not at first.

We arrived before they did and set up camp for a week of sun, sand, and surf. After the ten-hour drive from New Jersey, it felt heavenly to relax in our camp chairs while the boys played in their little inflatable pool. We liked our site, and the campground looked great for Max and Theo. It had an Olympic-size swimming pool, a hot tub, multiple playgrounds, clean bathhouses, and lots of friendly folks on every site. Neighbors said hello to us and made small talk about our twin boys as they passed by. There wasn't much privacy between sites at this resort-style KOA, and there was very little shade, but we knew that before we made reservations, so there were no surprises. Not for us. We were very happy and relaxed. Then Stephanie's mom and dad pulled up.

When her mother stepped out of the car and surveyed their campsite (which was right next to ours), she looked horrified. I wasn't sure what the problem was, but I knew there was a problem. And because we had picked the campground and the sites within the campground, I instantly felt guilty and responsible.

She was upset because the campsite was not private, and they would be in a tent all week. She was also disappointed because the campground looked nothing like Assateague State Park, where she was used to going for beach-camping trips. Instead of large, semiprivate sites surrounded by dunes and flowing seagrass, she was surrounded by huge RVs. The thing that bothered her the most was the barbed-wire fence directly to the right of her site—and the monstrously bedecked vacation homes that were lined up in a row right behind that fence. She felt like a bunch of strangers would literally and figuratively be looking down at her all week long.

"But what about the Olympic-size pool and the hot tub?" I muttered under my breath. I felt awful.

Stephanie's mom did get over her initial shock, but this was clearly not the place for her—even though Stephanie and I loved it there and would return again and again.

So who was right? Was it a great resort-style campground with amazing amenities? Or was it a field full of RVs without shade? It was both. We were both right. But we weren't both happy.

Six Tips for Camping with Family and Friends

So how do you avoid these types of camping conflicts with your family and friends? How do you find that location and campground that will make everyone happy? We all want to end up laughing around the campfire each night having the time of our lives, right? And nobody wants to end up on a camping trip with unhappy family members or unhappy friends.

Here are six great tips to ensure that you make magical memories at the campground with your family and friends. Time to pull up a camp chair and take some notes.

Tip #1: Choose a Campground Together

I had assumed that Stephanie's parents would love the Cape Hatteras KOA because we did, and Stephanie's parents had trusted that we would pick a place that they would love, because we'd all beach camped together in the past.

But when it comes to traveling with family and friends, one family should never completely entrust the other with making all of the decisions. Each family needs to research the campground and make sure that it's right for them. It may be complicated to hash this out beforehand, but doing so is preferable to showing up and being disappointed in someone else's choices—or having other people (especially your mother-in-law) be disappointed in yours.

In their heart of hearts, Stephanie's mom and dad are state park campers who really don't care about snack stands and swimming pools. But Stephanie and I love both rustic state park campgrounds *and* posh resort campgrounds. Because we wanted to camp with family on that

Cape Hatteras trip, we should have talked it all out beforehand and picked a state park. We could have saved the KOA resort experience for another time.

Some families love rustic public campgrounds, some love resort campgrounds, and some folks love both. Whatever category you fall into is just fine. Just make sure to know before you go, instead of showing up and being disappointed.

You also want to make sure to pick really good individual sites (and a good configuration of those sites) for your particular camping trip. Picking the campground is only half the battle, or half the fun, depending on how you look at it!

Tip #2: Arrange Your Sites Together as a Group

We love being able to camp with other families who don't own RVs. We have discovered that most campgrounds are well suited for diverse groups of campers with varying degrees of experience and equipment. Tent campers, RV owners, and cabin renters can all share a great outdoors vacation together at the same campground and often reserve sites that are close together or side by side. Some campgrounds do separate the tenting sites, cabin sites, and RV sites into different areas, but the current trend in the industry is to intermingle cabin sites and RV sites, so that multifamily groups can stay together.

A campground with tenting sites, RV sites, and cabin rentals also offers a wide variety of price points for prospective campers. A typical private campground might charge $30 to $40 a night for a tenting site, $50 to $80 a night for an RV site, and between $150 and $250 a night for a cabin. This allows families with very different budgets to camp together.

Some families may want sites right next to each other, and other families might like a little private space. If you want to camp right next to another family, you should ask campgrounds if they have buddy sites. Buddy sites are designed so that two RVs face each other (awning to awning), and there is a large common area in the middle with shared picnic tables and a shared fire ring. We loved getting buddy sites with Joe and Ashley, so that our kids could play together in the middle of the two RVs and we could easily share meals and campfires together, both before and after the kids went to bed.

Typical RV sites do not face each other awning to awning—instead, you usually end up facing the back side (the side without doors) of your neighbor's RV. This is more private and desirable when you are camping next to strangers, although you may occasionally end up with a view of your neighbors' sewer hookups and may see them emptying them (hopefully not Cousin Eddie style) while you are having dinner at your picnic table or relaxing in your camp chairs.

Consider that there may be situations where you do not want to be camping right next to your friends on buddy sites. I remember a summer when Max and Theo's bedtime was earlier than Izzy and Morgan's. When we put our boys to bed, they could hear their friends playing right outside of our RV. I had never seen such sullen and depressed looks on their faces before! They looked like they were prisoners in solitary confinement, not happy little boys at a campground!

To be honest, Stephanie and I had a few fights about bedtime that summer, but we eventually worked it all out. For the historical record, Stephanie probably would have been fine with letting them stay up later if they didn't like to wake up at 6:00 a.m. every morning, regardless of how late they went to bed. I probably shouldn't have picked buddy sites that summer.

My bad.

Choosing RV and tenting sites for a group trip is pretty easy work at most campgrounds. But now, more than ever, so is arranging a group trip with friends and family who don't own RVs and wouldn't dream of camping in a tent.

RV and tenting sites do tend to dominate the landscape at most campgrounds, but the market for alternative accommodations is growing. Many private campgrounds (and even some public ones) are adding dozens of cabins, glamping tents, yurts, A-frames, cabooses, treehouse rentals, on-site RV rentals, and much more. There has never been a more interesting time to take a family vacation at an American campground. We love going in our own RV, filled with our own linens, cookware, bikes, and fishing gear—but it must be said that ownership of an RV (or even ownership of a tent) is no longer required to take an epic camping vacation.

---------- **10 Great Campgrounds with Buddy Sites** ----------

- ✧ Yogi Bear's Jellystone Park in Quarryville, PA
- ✧ Yogi Bear's Jellystone Park in Williamsport, MD
- ✧ Lake-In-Wood Camping Resort in Narvon, PA
- ✧ Anchor Down RV Resort in Dandridge, TN
- ✧ Unicoi State Park and Lodge in Helen, GA
- ✧ Compass RV Resort in St. Augustine, FL
- ✧ Austin East KOA in Austin, TX
- ✧ San Francisco North/Petaluma KOA in Petaluma, CA
- ✧ Grand Canyon Railway RV Park in Williams, AZ
- ✧ Tucson/Lazydays KOA in Tucson, AZ

Tip #3: Plan Group Activities Together, but Don't Overplan Them

We love going on outdoor adventures with other families, and we occasionally plan those types of group activities together. Our boys have always loved hiking, but they love hiking with friends even more. They are lukewarm when it comes to kayaking, but if their friends are coming along, it quickly morphs into a great adventure. But it isn't always easy to hike or kayak with another family. Keeping multiple families on the same schedule can get tricky and stressful. If your family loves to get up early and go for a hike before the trail gets crowded, and another family likes to sleep in a little, it may be better to go separately and agree to meet up again later at the campground.

Over the years, we have learned the importance of building in flextime when we are camping with friends. If we are camping together for a weekend, we might plan a Saturday morning hike together and keep the rest of the weekend open. If we are spending the week camping with friends, we might plan joint activities every other day at most.

Flextime is key. No one wants to feel like they are being dragged around from one activity to another while on vacation. We all need to feel like we have choices at the campground. If you want to take a hike, take a hike. If you want to take a nap, take a nap. If you are traveling with kids, life can be unpredictable, and schedules and priorities can change quickly. If a cranky baby needs a nap or if someone is not feeling well, things can get stressful fast. Building flextime into your camping schedule makes it easy to deal with these issues as they come up.

It's also important to plan activities that are *just for your family*, even when you are on a multifamily trip. As a parent, I want to spend some vacation time alone with my spouse and kids in a relaxing environment. We have also learned that our kids benefit from downtime away from their friends, so that they don't end up exhausted and overstimulated. It is possible for your kids to have *too much fun* and then come crashing down from the emotional high of constant friend time. When you pull your kids away from their friends on a family camping trip to go out for dinner or do an activity without the other family, you may find that they whine because they want to keep playing. This has certainly happened to us, but we set our expectations and stuck to them. Our boys eventually learned that camping trips with friends would also include spending quality time with Mom and Dad.

It can be hard to strike this type of balance while vacationing with another family, but it can be disastrous if you don't. Ultimately, you may have friends who you love and adore but who do not make good traveling partners. But hopefully, you can find your own Ashley and Joe (and Izzy and Morgan!) to camp with. As I've mentioned, your kids will love you for taking them camping, and they will love you even more for taking them camping with friends! But life isn't just about making the kids happy, is it? Camping with friends also has awesome benefits for Mom and Dad.

Tip #4: Take Turns Watching Each Other's Kids

During one of our early camping trips with Ashley and Joe, an amazing thing happened that I will never forget. Joe walked up to me privately and asked if Stephanie and I would like to go out to dinner that night while they watched our kids—and then we could swap the next night and watch their kids while they went out to dinner. He seemed nervous to ask, but as soon as he did, my jaw dropped. It was brilliant! I felt like we were discovering some vast new country together. A brave new world where stressed out moms and dads could reconnect and go out on date nights while on vacation! I couldn't remember the last time that Stephanie and I had gone out on a date together. And the only thing that I had to do in return was watch Joe's well-behaved kids the next night? Sign me up! I also felt like I was snookering Joe in the bargain because I had three kids and he only had two. What a deal!

Soon after Joe's momentous camping epiphany, we were swapping babysitting duties all the time on our joint camping trips. Joe would quietly sidle up to me away from the womenfolk and ask if I wanted to go on a hike with Stephanie while he and Ashley watched the kids. I would immediately say yes and offer the same thing to him. We both looked at each other like we were mad geniuses who were single-handedly reinventing modern parenting. These "child swaps" were also amazing for Stephanie and me because they allowed us to go on adventurous hikes and kayak rides that we couldn't do with our own kids yet.

One of my greatest memories from this time period is of watching Izzy and Morgan while Ashley and Joe hiked the Beehive Loop trail in Acadia National Park, and then doing the same hike alone with Stephanie after they returned. The Beehive Loop crisscrosses the side of a very steep mountain and offers stunning views of the Atlantic Ocean and the beach below. I remember looking down from the top and seeing our boys as little specks. Two responsible parents were watching them play in the sand while Stephanie and I took in some of the most magnificent, sparkling water views on the Eastern Seaboard. For just a moment, we felt young and wild and free again, without a care in the world.

Then we hustled down the side of the mountain and reclaimed our children. It was getting close to dinnertime, and Stephanie was worried that the boys would be hungry soon. It was her turn to cook.

Tip #5: Discuss Meal Arrangements in Advance

When we camped with Ashley and Joe, we always did the meal planning before the trip. If it was a weekend trip, we would make one dinner and they would make one. The family that planned on showing up at the campground first on Friday night would always make that dinner, so that a hot meal would be waiting for the other family. Then the favor would be returned with a Saturday night dinner. I fondly remember several weekend camping trips were we got stuck in horrific traffic on a Friday night and didn't arrive at the campground until after 8:00 p.m. When we pulled into the campground, the boys were hangry and Stephanie and I were both still tense from the long drive. But then we unhitched the RV and walked over to Ashley's and Joe's site. Dinner was waiting, the campfire was roaring, and within minutes we were all relaxed and laughing and eating good food together.

For longer trips, like our weeklong trip to Acadia, we would often agree to make two dinners each for the other family. That would leave three dinners open for exploring the local food scene or just eating a quiet meal alone with our own kids. This system always worked perfectly for

both of our families. Taking complete responsibility for making a meal for another family (and getting one in return) has always worked better for us than making separate dishes and then combining them into one big multifamily potluck. We find that there are too many moving parts and that coordination and cleanup can get complicated. Plenty of campers love to do big potlucks—and that is just fine. It's all about finding your own mojo at the campground. Do what works for you.

Case in point, we typically have breakfast and lunch on our own when we camp with friends. Everyone wakes up at a slightly different time, and scheduling a big morning breakfast can often really slow down the beginning of a day. We like to get up and go early, so we can be the first ones at the trailhead each morning.

We also never schedule group lunches with another family. We are often out exploring during lunchtime, and we like to find awesome road-food joints while we are traveling. Eating lunch out is significantly cheaper than eating dinner out, and you can often get the same food. Roadside joints are also great places to bring little kids. They often have outdoor seating and a loud and bustling scene, so if your kids are also loud, no one will really notice. Traveling with a copy of Jane and Michael Stern's classic *Roadfood: An Eater's Guide to More Than 1,000 of the Best Local Hot Spots and Hidden Gems Across America* is highly recommended! We keep a copy in our truck.

Because we cook so many meals at our RV, we feel like we save enough money to justify eating out a few times. Sharing great meals with friends and finding great local food are two of our favorite activities when we go camping. Striking that perfect balance between scheduled campground meals and spontaneous roadside eats is a travel skill worth mastering.

Tip #6: Be Flexible with Your Co-Travelers and Expect Flexibility in Return

The single most important tip for traveling with friends and family is to be flexible and expect that flexibility in return, particularly if you are traveling with kids. Our everyday lives are heavy with schedules and obligations and responsibilities. A camping trip should be loose and mellow and fun. If one family is overplanning activities and strictly scheduling meals, that can quickly lead to tension and stress and miscommunication. If Stephanie and I ever wanted to switch up our plans or reschedule a meal because we found an awesome place to go kayaking, or if we ended up staying late exploring a nearby town, Ashley and Joe were always flexible about it. Being adventurous on a camping trip often means being spontaneous and following joy wherever it takes you.

If you follow these six tips for camping with family and friends, I can pretty much guarantee that you will have an awesome time at the campground. Now you just need to remember to communicate with the in-laws before each trip. Do the planning together or be willing to go it alone. You also need to find your own camping buddies. Your own Ashley and Joe. It's okay if you can't find camping buddies among your current friends. Just take a good look around. You'll see them at the campground.

W hen our twin boys were born, the honest truth is that our activity level plummeted fast. Even though we were making such an effort to have fun adventures, we were also constantly making decisions based on a simmering fear of getting caught in a tricky situation with little humans.

For the first couple of years, we were definitely spending a lot of time outdoors with the boys, but we would often do the safe or easier version of the activity at hand. I remember visiting the Lakota Wolf Preserve in our home state and taking the shuttle up to the top of the mountain, when in the past we had enjoyed the beautiful hike. When we visited the Delaware Water Gap, we just ate a picnic lunch instead of hiking up to Mount Tammany and soaking in those incredible views. Now, I'm not saying that those adjustments were necessarily a mistake. We did our best to get outside and have fun, even though we had a couple of new babies along for the ride. But I do think that there was an underlying current of nervousness and fear that held us back for our first couple of years as parents.

Acadia National Park helped me break through that fear. When Max and Theo were two and a half years old, we went on a two-week RV trip that culminated in one of my very favorite places in the entire world, Acadia National Park.

There's definitely an "easy" way to enjoy this park. You can hang out on the Park Loop Road and enjoy breathtaking views of Sand Beach and Thunder Hole along with hundreds of other tourists. But in the past, we had always loved the quiet parts of Acadia, where you could hike and bike for miles and not see another living soul. Acadia National Park brought out my determination to stop holding myself back from having those exhilarating, awe-inspiring moments just because I had become a mother. I decided that I could be brave and bold without being reckless and unsafe. So we bought a couple of hiking backpacks, strapped those toddlers in, and hiked the Great Head Trail on our first day in Acadia National Park.

In many ways, my story as a mom can be separated into two phases: before the Great Head Trail hike and after the Great Head Trail hike. I'll always remember scrambling up a rock with a two-year-old on my back and thinking that it was the most fun I'd had in years. I felt like a world of possibilities was opening up in front of me. It sounds dramatic, but I think that hike helped me believe that parenting could truly be a great adventure—but it was up to me to be brave enough to make that happen.

I've never forgotten the giddy excitement that I felt that day. My body ached from carrying the weight of that toddler on my back for miles, and that was the best kind of soreness I could imagine. Our family adventures changed after that. I became more willing to try new things with the boys like boat tours, biking, kayaking, and zip-lining. Not every new adventure was a success, but at least we made the effort and, of course, learned some lessons for the next time.

I gained confidence on that amazing trip to Acadia National Park, but I still tried to be smart about trying new activities with our young children. Nevertheless, there have been plenty of mishaps along the way. Wesley, our youngest, is apparently petrified of canoes. We didn't discover this until we were out in the middle of Lake Crescent in Olympic National Park. We all made it safely back to shore, but that epic meltdown remains one of our funniest family memories to date.

Basic Guidelines for Adventures with Little Ones

There are plenty of things you can't predict or plan for when it comes to family travel, but we've developed some guidelines that help us maximize the adventure and minimize the drama.

Be Smart about the Schedule

Our three boys aren't babies anymore, but we still think that respecting their natural schedule is one of the most important ways to keep these campers happy. If we are trying a new activity as a family, I make sure to do it at our best time of the day. If you have kids who nap, you're inviting a catastrophe by scheduling a kayak tour at that time. Think about when your kids normally eat or sleep and keep those times sacred, even when traveling.

Downtime Is Important Too!

The campground is the perfect place to enjoy card and board games.

Here are some classics that our boys love:

- checkers
- Uno
- Yahtzee
- Skip-Bo
- spit

And some new favorites:

- Spot It!
- Sushi Go!
- 5 Second Rule
- Heads Up!
- The Oregon Trail Card Game

Our boys are long past their napping years, but they are still happier and better behaved in the morning. By late afternoon, no matter where we are or what we are doing, they are ready for serious downtime at the campsite. That might change in the future, but for now, sunset boat rides are off the table.

Have an Exit Strategy

If you are a parent, you know that anything can go wrong at any time. With three kids, we pretty much expect some sort of hiccup in any plan that we make. Even though I love trying new things with the boys, I always consider what our exit strategy will be if something unexpected happens. If someone gets sick or hurt, how can we get out of the situation?

Some activities, like boat rides or cave tours, place you in an environment with limited exit options. I avoided situations like this until I knew that we were pretty well past the constant-bathroom-breaks stage of life. On guided tours, I like to make sure that we can safely remove ourselves from the group if one of our kids starts acting up. And even though we love public transportation, we always opt to take our own vehicle so we can get out of Dodge fast, even if it means paying more for parking in a downtown area.

Bring Snacks

If you want to have exciting and successful adventures with your kids, the most important thing to know is that you should never, ever go anywhere without food. Hungry kids are miserable kids. Even if you think you are going for the shortest outing in the history of outings, bring snacks. Some of our worst travel moments involved situations where I had nothing to feed my hangry children.

The simple truth is that finding healthy but yummy snacks will help your kids be better travel buddies. At my best moments, I have trail mix, cheese and crackers, apples with peanut butter, and other foods that give them energy without a corresponding sugar high. But in all honesty, there was a period of time when our youngest child enjoyed almost every family hike with a bag of Skittles in his hand. It worked for us, so we went with it. You do you.

Provide a Challenge

After a few years of family travel, we realized something very interesting. The more challenged our kids were physically, the better behaved they were. If we were on a simple, flat hike in the woods, our boys would be fighting each other with sticks and asking how much farther we had to go. As soon as we introduced rock scrambles, bridges, or steep climbs, they got focused and intense. When we treat our kids as if they are a little bit older and a little bit more mature, they usually rise to the challenge and act like it.

This doesn't just apply to physical activity. We've taken a lot of guided tours with our kids, and that's not always an easy thing to do. But we've found that our boys are so much more engaged when they are listening to an expert on a topic. We've toured caves in the Black Hills of South Dakota; the historic district in Charleston, South Carolina; and the Naval Academy in Annapolis, Maryland. Once when I was buying tickets at the Alamo in Texas, the guide looked at our children and informed me that the tour would probably be uninteresting to "young guests." I passed his thoughts along to my boys, and they stayed at the front of the group for the entire hour, asking him questions at every stop along the tour. I'm pretty sure they felt insulted, and they were up for the challenge of proving him wrong.

The Magic of Rock Painting!

Do you have an artistic or crafty kid? Rock painting has been gaining in popularity at campgrounds around the country. Kids paint rocks and hide them. Then they look for and collect rocks that have been painted by other campers. Follow these five steps to create and share your own painted rocks:

1. Find and collect small, flat rocks that will be easy to paint.
2. Paint the top of the rock however you like. Some people have a "signature" design and others paint regional or camping scenes.
3. Write a message on the back for whoever finds your rock. Some people write an email address. You can also write the name of a rock-painting Facebook group like RVing Rocks!
4. Hide your rocks for other campers to find.
5. Look for rocks that other campers have painted and hidden.

Respect Your Child's Fears and Anxieties, but Don't Pass On Your Own Phobias

My father was a member of the "throw the kids in the pool and they'll learn to swim" school of parenting. I vividly remember him taking me outside in the midst of a massive summer storm to cure me of my fear of lightning. Let's just say I decided to do things a little differently with my own kids.

It is certainly challenging to find a balance between encouraging your children to try new things and respecting their boundaries. The first time I took my boys zip-lining, I refused to give them that gentle push off the ledge because I wanted them to make the choice themselves. Instead, I jumped off the ledge first, turned my body around, and waved at them to follow. My heart almost burst with joy when they did follow, one at a time.

I'll never force my children to do something that scares them, but I will let them see me do it and encourage them to join in on the fun. On the flip side, I try very hard not to pass along my own fears. I have always been prone to claustrophobia, and Jeremy is terrified of heights. Both of us have worked very hard to overcome those anxieties so we won't pass on our own limiting beliefs to our children.

Do the Touristy Stuff

Before I had kids, I might have been a little bit of a travel snob. I was one of those people who thrived on finding the off-the-beaten-path treasures in a popular destination. While I still love to quiz local residents and discover hidden gems, I've also embraced the value of well-known tourist traps. We're still fairly picky about which ones we visit, but road-tripping has taught us that just because places like Wall Drug in South Dakota, Santa's Village in New Hampshire, and Dollywood in Tennessee are well-known and popular doesn't necessarily mean that they are overrated. They are actually a whole lot of fun. Take the time to enjoy the simple, touristy pleasures when traveling with kids.

Invest in the Gear You Need to Have Adventures with Your Kids

I can be a bit of a skinflint with big-ticket items, so I have to admit that I missed out on some fun when the twins were young because I didn't want to spend money on gear. It took me two years to finally buy hiking backpacks for the kids, and I seriously regret not making the investment earlier. Another purchase I held back on was a bike trailer. I wasn't sure if we would use it often enough to make the purchase worthwhile. We missed out on countless bike rides because of this. Once our youngest was born, I finally bit the bullet and bought a bike seat for him. That was one of the best baby purchases we made. Another piece of gear that was worth its weight in gold was a truly rugged double jogging stroller. The price tag almost made me pass out with shock, but our BOB two-seater was a beloved member of our family for seven years.

Here are a few simple truths about spending money on kid gear. First, you can find most things lightly used at a great price. Second, anything that supports your family getting outside is worth the investment. And third, you can resell it when you are done using it. Unfortunately I didn't understand these truths until my third child, but I'm glad I finally realized that the cost of this gear was an investment in our family.

Spend Money When It Matters

As teachers, we always had the time to travel but not necessarily the money. Our vacations were usually very budget-oriented, and we always took advantage of any free activities available. A few splurges over the years taught me that some of those more expensive ticketed adventures are worth the cost.

So how do you tell the difference between expensive experiences that just blow the vacation budget and ones that are worth every penny? We tend to only splurge on truly regional experiences, where we feel that the activity or event captures the magic of a particular destination. Examples of these type of experiences are the dune-buggy tour at the Cape Cod National Seashore; Diver Ed's Dive-In Theater in Bar Harbor, Maine; and the hayride and chuckwagon cookout in Custer State Park Resort, South Dakota. These were all a bit of a stretch for our traveling budget, but they brought the areas to life, and we will remember them for years to come.

Great Outdoor Activities with Kids

How have we expanded our horizons as a family while road-tripping and camping around the country? As mentioned previously, we always look for adventures that are unique to a certain region, like whale watching or dune climbing. But there are certain activities that are easy to enjoy whether you are in the Pacific Northwest or the Carolina Low Country. We've worked particularly hard to get our boys on board with outdoor activities that we can enjoy at a relatively low cost, no matter where we are camping. Here are some beginner tips for our favorite family hobbies.

Most Popular Activities among Campers

1. Hiking
2. Fishing
3. Canoeing/kayaking
4. Scenic drives and sightseeing
5. Biking
6. Visiting historical sites

(KOA, 2019 North American Camping Report)

Hiking

Many people who aren't big hikers start doing it a lot more once they begin camping. Our camping lifestyle seems to place us in the proximity of amazing hikes all the time. There are often trails right in the campground or nearby in a state or national park. Hiking is good for all ages and ability levels. Plus, it's practically free, aside from some costs for gear and occasional park entrance fees. If you want to start hiking with your kids, here are five pieces of advice that we've learned over the years:

---------- **Geocaching: A Modern-Day Treasure Hunt** ----------

Geocaching is an outdoor treasure-hunting game where players use GPS-enabled devices to find a geocache container hidden at a certain location. People often leave small tokens or mementos for other folks to find. It's a fun and free activity. Want to try it?

1. Go to www.geocaching.com or download the free Geocaching app to create an account.

2. Locate a geocache near your location on the app.

3. Use a GPS device to find the cache.

4. Fill out the logbook.

5. If you take a piece of "treasure," leave another item behind for the next geocacher to find!

1 **Be smart and prepared.** We've seen people heading out on trails with no maps, no water, and no knowledge of wildlife safety protocols. Even on trails that are rated as easy or beginner level, it's important to have the proper gear and wear appropriate clothing. Remember, you're not at Disney World.

2 **Talk to the experts.** We do a lot of trip planning and research before we show up at a destination, but we don't act like know-it-alls. We talk to campground owners or camp hosts to get insider information on any trails that we plan on exploring. At state and national parks, we always stop in and talk to rangers before a hike. Often they will have up-to-date intel on trail conditions that isn't available anywhere else.

3 **Take on a challenge and do more than "walk in the woods."** We've found that the best family hikes include a bit of a physical challenge for our kids. They love hikes with bridges, rungs, and ladders. Rock scrambling is always a big hit. Hiking for a few miles on flat ground through the woods? Never a success.

4 **Find a water feature.** It turns out that even the smallest creek can be a really fun treat when hiking with kids. We search out hikes with waterfalls, rivers, lakes, and ponds, since these are always a favorite. Make sure to pack appropriate footwear and a change of clothes, though, since most kids love to get wet and then complain about being wet.

5 **Use the AllTrails app.** The AllTrails app is available for iOS or Android devices and offers a comprehensive library of data for hikes across America. We love the detailed maps and hike reviews from app users. The free version has always suited our needs just fine, but you can upgrade to the Pro version if you want to download hiking maps for use offline and access additional app features.

Kayaking and Canoeing

Kayaking is something that we really embraced once we started camping because we love finding campgrounds near the ocean, lakes, or bays. Before we bought our first pop-up camper, we had done a few guided kayak tours that were just magical to us. We figured that for the cost of one guided tour, we could buy a kayak of our own. But we highly recommend beginning with a guided tour first. This will give you an idea of whether you really love the activity. Plus, the guides usually give a brief but very helpful lesson. Here are some of our four tips on enjoying kayaking and canoeing with your family:

1 **Seriously consider renting instead of buying.** Many places where we have camped offer rentals or are close to locations where you can rent. Many state and national parks have rental concessionaires on-site as well. Crunch the numbers, or maybe try renting for one year of camping and see if you spend enough time and money to make it worth having your own.

2 **Don't overspend if you decide to buy your own.** There are very fancy and expensive kayaks and canoes out there, and most of us hobbyists just don't need all those bells and whistles. We bought two very affordable kayaks from the Ascend line at Bass Pro Shops and Cabela's. They've served us well for years, and we're glad we didn't blow the budget on them.

3 **Do a little research on inflatable kayaks.** We've talked to quite a few campers who have been very happy with their inflatable Sea Eagles. This is such a great option for folks who are tight on space and don't want to bother with storage and racks.

4 **Be safe.** We are very careful to model safe water-sports behavior for our boys, and we've required them to always wear life jackets from day one. We also talk to locals before we put our kayak in at an unfamiliar place. Just like hiking, you want to know what lies ahead.

> Young campers say that fishing and hiking are their favorite camping activities, followed by biking, sightseeing, and canoeing.
>
> *(KOA, 2019 North American Camping Report)*

Cave Exploration

You might be surprised by how many opportunities there are for cave exploration all around the country. For kids, there is something incredibly magical about heading underground and seeing the world in a whole new way. We went on an epic three-week road trip in the Pacific Northwest, and our boys will tell you that their single favorite day of the whole vacation was hiking in the lava tubes around Mount St. Helens. They've also been in caves in Virginia and the Black Hills of South Dakota. Taking our kids underground grabs their attention every time. Here are four things to remember:

1. **Research the type of tours or hikes available.** Many cave sites offer a variety of tours, and it's important to find a good match for your family. In the Ape Caves of Washington State, we chose the easier lava-tube hike that didn't include any tight spaces. Some cave tours don't allow strollers or baby carriers. Many will have age guidelines.

2. **Check the tour schedule.** Many, if not most, caves have some restrictions on public access. Places like Mammoth Cave National Park in Kentucky and Wind Cave National Park in South Dakota require tickets to tour the caves. The reservation process varies from park to park and can be complicated, so definitely do some advance research.

3. **Take baby steps.** You cannot know in advance how your child will react to going underground. Tread carefully and start with larger, well-lit caves. We carried extra flashlights for our youngest when we hiked the Ape Caves because we know he is a bit nervous in the dark.

4. **Dress appropriately.** Caves remain a fairly steady temperature that's usually close to the annual average temperature of the cave's location. So there are caves in Texas with a year-round temperature of seventy degrees, while the ones in Mammoth Cave are around fifty-four degrees. We always make sure to dress in layers and bring along some extra sweatshirts. You'll also want to pay attention to footwear restrictions. As part of the effort to combat white-nose syndrome, a disease that is decimating bat populations in the United States, many cave sites will not allow you to wear shoes that you wore in any other cave.

Junior Ranger Programs

Junior Ranger booklets are available at national parks, national seashores, and national historic sites across the country. The booklets contain activities that are specific to that location, and children can earn badges or patches for completing the park booklets. Most Junior Ranger programs are free of charge, but a few parks like Yellowstone do charge a nominal fee for the booklets. These programs have captured our boys' imaginations all over the country, from Olympic National Park to Sleeping Bear Dunes to FDR's home in Hyde Park, New York. This is an amazing way to get your kids excited about visiting our nation's natural and historic treasures. If you're interested in the programs, consider these four tips:

1. **Do some advance research.** We like to look online or call to see what the general Junior Ranger requirements are for a particular park. Sometimes our visit will be too short to complete the program, and we like to know that in advance. For example, we only had about four hours at Crater Lake National Park in Oregon, and we knew that we wanted to do the rim hike. So we let the kids know ahead of time that we wouldn't be earning Junior Ranger badges that day.

2 **Pick up your Junior Ranger booklet before doing anything else in the national park.** Every Junior Ranger booklet is different, so we like to know the requirements before we start hopping around a park. Often the booklets will require attendance at a ranger talk or two, so it's good to get the schedule and plan that at the beginning of your visit.

3 **Celebrate the swearing-in ceremony.** Our boys earned their very first Junior Ranger badges at Cape Hatteras National Seashore. We took pictures and made a big fuss, then celebrated with ice cream. We wanted them to look forward to collecting even more badges and patches in the future.

4 **Check out the online Junior Ranger programs that can be completed from home.** If your kids really connect with this type of learning, the National Park Service (NPS) has programs that you can complete at home when you aren't camping. Topics include fishing, exploring the wilderness, and learning about the night sky. Once they've completed the activities, you mail them in to receive the badge.

⌗

If we want our kids to be excited about the outdoors, we have to embrace the adventure. Depending on your kids, that might mean splurging on ziplining or just tracking down amazing fishing holes. Every child is going to respond to and connect with different activities. On every single camping trip, we challenge ourselves as parents to convince our boys that the natural world is more exciting than anything they can find on their screens and devices. That's a tall order, but it's worth the effort. For every new destination we explore, I think about how I can challenge my kids to enjoy the beauty of nature. If I can get them to say *wow*, whether it's when we're gazing at a cascading waterfall or climbing through a pitch-black cave, it's been a good day of family travel in my book.

A few years before the boys were born, Stephanie and I went on a five-day trip to Acadia National Park. It was late August, right before we both had to report back to work at our respective teaching jobs. We stayed in a romantic little bed-and-breakfast right outside the park gates. Looking back, it seems like another life. We had so much time on our hands before the kids were born, and frankly, I'm not really sure what we did with all of it. Thankfully, we had both developed an interest in visiting our national parks in a more intentional way, and Acadia was within striking distance of our home in New Jersey. So we packed up our little car and went. The other great national parks of the American West seemed so far away back then, almost like they were on another planet. So for us, it was Acadia or bust.

We had no idea that this trip would end up changing our lives. Each morning began with coffee and a quick breakfast followed by a trip to the NPS visitor center to grab a map or consult the rangers about a hike. Each afternoon was filled with rocky scrambles and stunning ocean vistas. Each evening ended with a kayak ride and a lobster roll in Bar Harbor. I remember going to bed with sore arms and legs every night because of all the

> Campers spend about one in every five camping nights at a national park campground.
>
> *(KOA, 2019 North American Camping Report)*

hiking and paddling. The exhaustion felt great. So we got up each morning and did it again—and pushed ourselves a bit further.

Acadia's combination of pink granite ledges and windswept seas was mesmerizing. I felt like I could spend my life hiking there and never get bored. It was hard to believe that this was just one of our country's great national parks and that there were so many more of them out there to explore and discover. I wanted to visit them all and I think that Stephanie felt the same way. We both wondered aloud why we had never been to Yellowstone or Yosemite—and we promised each other that we would get to them. That we would get to *all of them*.

We fell in love with Acadia on that trip and also with the entire ethos of our national park system. In retrospect, I think that trip formed an essential chapter in our family's shared origin story, even though the boys were not born yet. Because in a sense, Stephanie and I were reborn in Acadia. We had spent years taking lazy beach vacations in Cape Hatteras and road-tripping to music festivals in Asheville and New Orleans—and we always had our fun. But this trip to Acadia was different. More exciting. More fulfilling. We had fallen in love with something that needed our nurturing and protecting—but that was also, in a strange way, nurturing and protecting us back. It felt like we had just been informed of a surprise inheritance that we never knew was coming—and we didn't want to squander it.

When we bought our first RV, we knew where we really wanted to take our boys. The vision we both had was about camping and getting outside wherever and whenever we could, but it was also about our national parks. We wanted to show our sons the awe-inspiring magnificence of our country's "best idea." Simply put, we wanted to become a national park family and share our inheritance with them, because we knew that it was also theirs to claim. Stephanie and I had waited far too long to immerse ourselves in the national parks. We wanted to start the boys young.

So we did.

In recent years, we have gazed into the eyes of bison that were standing just steps away from our truck in Badlands National Park, and we have pulled up our pant legs and waded out to the base of rushing waterfalls in Olympic National Park. We have crossed the Oconaluftee River on wooden footbridges while hiking the Kephart Prong Trail in Great Smoky Mountains National Park, and we have climbed over the majestic fallen trunks of two-thousand-year-old redwood trees in the park in Northern California that bears their name. And we have done these things together.

The wildness and freedom that can be found in these parks are the perfect antidote to the stress and anxiety of living in our claustrophobic digital age. Our national park trips have nourished our souls and astonished our senses. But they have also humbled us.

Why?

Because national parks can be difficult to navigate and downright dangerous. They can also be intimidating in their size and scope. They need to be approached with wonder and awe—but also with a sense of respect. Do you want to road trip with your kids to Yellowstone and Yosemite or hike with them in Glacier and the Grand Canyon? Do you hear the mountains and the monuments and the seashores and the lakeshores calling? Then you simply must go.

Here's what you need to know!

Eight Tips for Enjoying
Our National Parks

Tip #1: Book Early if You Want to Stay in
NPS Lodges and Campgrounds

We recently tried to reserve a room in a Glacier National Park lodge. It was eleven months before our trip—and they were completely sold out. The concessioner-run lodges within our national parks are notoriously difficult to book, and we were forced, like so many others, to find accommodations outside of the park in a less scenic locale.

Several years ago, when we wanted to camp at the ever-popular Platte River Campground in Sleeping Bear Dunes National Lakeshore, I remember waking up at dawn and positioning myself before the computer, praying that I would be able to get a site when the booking window opened up that morning. My research from the day before showed that there were only seven sites available on the day of our arrival. I felt like I was locked in a battle royale with dozens of greedy families who also wanted my site. Thankfully, I nabbed one. It was a little closer to the bathhouse than we normally like. But I counted my blessings and thanked the camping gods for granting us a site.

The tip here is a simple one. If you want reservations for a popular national park lodge or campground, you need to book early. Way early. You need to find out how early reservations open up (sometimes it's six months, nine months, or twelve months before arrival) and get out your laptop or call at that exact moment. Not on that exact day, but at the exact hour when reservations open. The reservation websites that are used by many state and national park campgrounds are far from sophisticated and can be notoriously difficult to navigate. If you want to nab that perfect site (or even one right next to the bathhouse!), you'd better get ready to pour yourself a strong cup of coffee and put on your Captain Internet cape. You're gonna need it.

Tip #2: Get the Kids Educated and Excited before You Go!

Happiness scholars (yes, there is such a thing!) believe that the happiness derived from anticipating a trip can be greater than the happiness we experience on the trip itself. In the months leading up to a camping trip, we like to immerse ourselves and our kids in books, movies, videos, and music about the areas that we will be visiting. Before our road trip to Mount Rushmore last year, we bought the boys several books about the memorial and found a few others at the library. They read them all cover to cover.

YouTube also proved to be a terrific resource for fun little videos about Mount Rushmore, Crazy Horse, Wall Drug, chuckwagon dinners in the Black Hills, and bison watching in Badlands National Park. As the boys learned more about each destination, they started to develop opinions about our itinerary. We always encourage this and try to empower them by implementing their suggestions for hikes, activities, and even restaurants. This kind of autobiographical planning works wonders for the development of a child's imagination, and it's a great way to pass the hours on dreary winter weekends. This type of immersive and anticipatory learning is also a great way to teach our children to use digital technology in positive and proactive ways.

------ Children's and YA Books about our National Parks ------

* *The Wolf Keepers* by Elise Broach
* *The Camping Trip That Changed America: Theodore Roosevelt, John Muir, and Our National Parks* by Barb Rosenstock and Mordicai Gerstein
* *National Parks of the U.S.A.* by Kate Siber and Chris Turnham
* *National Parks: A Kid's Guide to America's Parks, Monuments, and Landmarks* by Erin McHugh and Neal Aspinall
* *Junior Ranger Activity Book: Puzzles, Games, Facts, and Tons More Fun Inspired by the U.S. National Parks!* by National Geographic Kids

Tip #3: Transcend TripAdvisor and Generic Guidebooks

Some campers feel overwhelmed and ill prepared when they visit our national parks. These travelers also feel disappointed when their Emersonian dream of time spent alone in nature crashes into the reality of full parking lots, crowded trailheads, and bustling vistas. To find your own slice of national park bliss, and to avoid national park burnout, we recommend that you look past many of the hikes, activities, and restaurants that are featured prominently on TripAdvisor and in the widely available guidebook series that attempt to cover all aspects of the parks in one volume. Why? Because more often than not, they all recommend the same five hikes, the same five activities, and the same five restaurants. No wonder those spots are all so crowded...

I'm not suggesting that you skip Old Faithful when you visit Yellowstone or bypass Park Loop Road when you visit Acadia. But I am suggesting that our parks offer so much more than any top-five list can contain. When planning a national park trip, you need to dig a little deeper. Get more detailed guidebooks that focus on the specific activities that you want to do while you are in the park.

If you want to hike in Yosemite, get a book that is specifically about hiking in Yosemite. If you want to go bird-watching in the Everglades, get a book that is about bird-watching in the Everglades. If you want to find the best places to take pictures in Acadia, then get a book about photography in Acadia. These types of books, often published by smaller presses, will include all of the popular spots mentioned in Fodor's and Frommer's, but they will also offer dozens of alternatives that might work better for your family anyway.

------ **Eight Amazing Family Hikes in our National Parks** ------

1. Hurricane Hill Trail, Olympic National Park
2. Gorham Mountain Trail, Acadia National Park
3. Kephart Prong Trail, Great Smoky Mountains National Park
4. Hiouchi Trail to Stout Grove, Jedediah Smith Redwoods State Park
5. Notch Trail, Badlands National Park
6. Empire Bluff Trail, Sleeping Bear Dunes National Lakeshore
7. Stony Man hike, Shenandoah National Park
8. Natural Entrance Tour, Wind Cave National Park (guided)

Tip #4: Let Park Rangers Put the Finishing Touches on Your Itinerary

We start every national park adventure with a trip to the visitor center and a talk with a ranger. We share our planned itinerary of hikes and activities with them and ask if we should make any adjustments. We almost always end up tweaking our plans based on the personal recommendations of the ranger. They may guide us away from a hike that is either too easy or too dangerous, or they might push us toward one that we missed in our research.

When we stopped into the Oconaluftee Visitor Center on the North Carolina side of Great Smoky Mountains National Park, I had several possible hikes in mind for that day. I mentioned each of them to a ranger. He was not particularly enthusiastic about the options I had selected. He asked me a few questions about the kids' hiking ability and whether they would be afraid to cross a few narrow wooden bridges that only had handrails on one side. We told him that they were strong and adventurous hikers. He handed me a map and circled the trailhead for the Kephart Prong Trail. He told me that we would love this hike and sent us on our way. It ended up being one of the five greatest family hikes that we have ever completed—and it wasn't in any of our guidebooks.

Time and time again, we have had rangers take a look at our family, ask us a few questions about our hiking or swimming ability, and point us toward incredible adventures with a well-marked map in hand. If you tell a ranger how far you like to hike and describe the ability level of each member of your group, you are pretty much guaranteed to get an incredible, highly personalized recommendation.

Thank you, rangers!

- - - - - - - - -   Best Apps for Exploring our National Parks   - - - - - - - - -

- ✧ National Parks by Chimani
- ✧ REI National Park Guide & Maps
- ✧ Oh, Ranger! ParkFinder
- ✧ Passport: Your National Parks
- ✧ Pocket Ranger National Park Passport Guide

Tip #5: Check for Amphitheater Talks, Interpretive Walks, and Junior Ranger Programs

After we talk to a ranger for personal recommendations, we make sure we have an accurate schedule for the amphitheater talks and interpretive walks that are taking place during our stay. Many national parks have amphitheaters for evening talks with a ranger, and if they do, we make sure to catch as many as we can. We have learned about the lives of otters and weasels in Sleeping Bear Dunes, about bird migrations in Acadia National Park, and about the stars and constellations in Badlands National Park. These ranger-led talks are always an absolute highlight for our children and for us. They are rarely crowded, and the rangers always make themselves available for questions after the talk. The amphitheaters are often right next door to the campgrounds, which means that we can walk there after dinner and walk back to our site after the talk.

We also love taking interpretive walks led by park rangers. We have learned about the early years of Theodore Roosevelt on a walk at the base of Mount Rushmore and searched for fossils with a park ranger in the

Badlands. A park ranger from Boston with a background in theater once guided us through a dramatic cave walk in Wind Cave National Park that none of us will ever forget. The climax of this walk came when the ranger silenced all of us and shut off his lantern so that we were all surrounded by absolute darkness and absolute silence.

I made sure to hold Wesley's hand. Or rather, I made sure that he held mine...

At the beginning of each national park adventure, we also make sure to grab the Junior Ranger booklets so our boys can earn their badges. For more information about this awesome program, check out Chapter Fifteen.

Every Kid in a Park

Did you know that fourth graders and their families can visit hundreds of national parks, lands, and waters free of charge? Here's how the program works:

- Go online to everykidinapark.gov and complete the "adventure diary."
- Print your pass.
- You can exchange the printed pass for a more durable one at certain federal park locations.
- Enjoy amazing park adventures all year for *free!*

Tip #6: Head to the Most Popular Destinations Early

There has been much ballyhoo in the media about the overcrowding and underfunding of our national parks. The underfunding part of the story is absolutely true. As of December 2018, our national parks were suffering through an $11.6 billion maintenance backlog. The infrastructure of our parks is desperately in need of repair and updating. But the "overcrowding" part of the typical media narrative has been oversimplified and has created some false impressions about our national parks.

Our most popular parks can definitely get overcrowded—but usually only during peak season, at peak hours, in their most iconic locations.

We have heard visitors complain for years about overcrowding in Acadia National Park—but in our extensive experience there, we have only experienced crowds along the ever-popular Park Loop Road during peak hours in the summer and fall. If you want to take a hike in Acadia and be all alone in the middle of a gorgeous summer day, you only have to venture a few miles off the beaten track. Or you can just get up really early like we do.

In park after park, we have discovered that most visitors don't really find their way to the trailheads or parking lots until 9:00 a.m or later. We try to get to popular spots before 8:00 a.m., and we always find parking—and rarely find crowds. But we do usually find crowds when we come back down off the trail before lunch. The parking lot that was empty three hours earlier is usually packed to the brim with cars, and many of them are parked illegally in unmarked spots.

Everyone else must be having more fun at night than we are. A wild night for us usually ends at about 11:15 p.m. and includes leftovers heated up over the campfire and no more than a glass of wine for Stephanie and an organic iced tea for me!

As we walk back to our truck, we are often semi-stalked by would-be hikers in cars who can't find parking spots for their Outbacks and 4Runners. Little do they know that it takes us at least fifteen to twenty minutes to load the kids in the truck—and that there is probably at least one kiddo who desperately needs to visit the restroom.

Tip #7: Spend Your Afternoons Off the Beaten Track

If you head to crowded national park destinations during peak hours each day, you will burn out quickly. At that point, you might as well be battling through the crowds at a theme park in Orlando. Heading to the most popular spots early in the morning is super important, but so is heading to off-the-beaten-track destinations during peak hours. After we knock out a hike in the morning, we often grab an early lunch and head back out into the park. But this time we head to a hike or swimming spot that is not mentioned in most of the major national guidebooks. This is where we lean

heavily on local knowledge, ranger recommendations, and the more specific guidebooks that we mentioned earlier. You can look for these more
granular guidebooks in the visitor center's bookstore. They almost always
stock them.

We call our morning and afternoon strategy #winning, and we follow
it day after day during our national park adventures. Later in the afternoon, we always head back to the campground to relax and recover. We are
always rested up for the next day. Needless to say, we never go home feeling
burned out. We go home craving more.

Gear for Hiking in our National Parks

- hiking backpack
- comfortable hiking boots
- emergency medical kit
- emergency whistle
- map and compass
- knife or multi-tool
- appropriate clothing (rain gear, warm layers, etc.)
- food and water

Tip #8: Take Safety Recommendations Seriously

Our national parks are wild places. They are not theme parks, even though
the crowds at popular spots can make them feel that way. Theme parks
manufacture an imagined sense of danger. Our national parks can actually
be dangerous, particularly for the unprepared. We always visit the park's
website and read the safety guidelines and recommendations before each
trip. Visitors need to be aware of risks related to wildlife and landscape.
When visiting the Great Smokies or Glacier, everyone should know how
to respond if they see a bear. When visiting the Badlands or Yellowstone,
everyone should be aware of the dangers of wandering off the trail into

unmarked terrain. Each park has its own unique set of risks, and thankfully, the NPS does a great job of educating visitors about how to avoid them.

Take the time to read up about safety concerns before venturing into any of our national parks. It could save your life or the lives of the ones you love.

You should also pay attention to signs while you are in the park. If a sign tells you to avoid approaching wildlife, then don't approach the wildlife. If a sign warns you that a hike is dangerous, then think twice about doing it. Be honest about your physical condition and preparedness. You shouldn't be afraid to have adventures in our national parks, but you should be well informed about them.

I think your family is well on its way to becoming a national park family, even if they don't know it yet. My only question is, which park will you fall in love with first?

Beyond the National Parks!

Don't forget! Our sixty-one national parks are all well worth visiting, but so are many other federal units that fall under a variety of different, and often confusing, designations. Many are every bit as spectacular as their more famous siblings.

National memorials—If you only visited NPS units that are designated as national parks, you would miss out on classic road-trip destinations such as Mount Rushmore National Memorial, which is tiny compared to Yellowstone or Yosemite—but every bit as iconic.

National battlefields (like Antietam) and *national military parks* (like Gettysburg) serve as historical feasts for Civil War buffs and casual tourists alike.

National recreation areas offer world-class hiking, kayaking, and fishing. The Delaware Water Gap, less than two hours from both New York City and Philadelphia, is just one great example.

National seashores—Many families make annual pilgrimages to NPS units like Cape Hatteras National Seashore for miles upon miles of wild, windswept beaches and the best surfing on the East Coast.

National lakeshores—Our national lakeshores, such as Sleeping Bear Dunes, are every bit as stunning as our most famous national parks. This underrated Michigan gem was voted "Most Beautiful Place in America" by viewers of *Good Morning America* in 2011.

National parkways such as the Blue Ridge Parkway, which links Shenandoah National Park to Great Smoky Mountains National Park, are worthy destinations in their own right. Plan on making plenty of stops, as stunning vistas and endless wildflowers abound.

CHAPTER

Seventeen

CREATING *and*
CAPTURING

Camping Memories

STEPHANIE

Years ago, when we had just started blogging about our family camping adventures, we got a surprisingly cranky comment on a post. A reader wrote that it was a complete waste of time and money to be having all of these adventures with our young twins "since they wouldn't remember any of it anyway."

Hmm.

My first response was a bit of an eye roll. We all do things with our young kids every single day that they won't remember years from now. They probably won't remember the first stories we read them or the lullabies we sing before bed. But most of us believe that all that stuff matters anyway, and it helps them grow up feeling loved, secure, and happy. Similarly, Jeremy and I always believed that we were training our little guys to be future road warriors. We wanted to instill a love of nature and an appreciation for exploring the world long before they could actually remember our family camping trips.

But beyond that, our children aren't the only ones who matter in this family travel equation. Even though our twin boys don't remember that first camping trip to a scrubby state park in South Jersey, I can remember every detail like it was yesterday. We immediately started creating amazing memories for ourselves as parents, and I am forever grateful for that. I love the fact that our family identity includes countless moments spent together around the campfire. We've celebrated birthdays and holidays at the campground, and those memories might be fleeting for the kids, but they are bright and vivid for us as parents.

Now, many years later, I understand something else. My kids remember far more than I ever imagined they would. My older sons talk in detail about a boat tour we took in Bar Harbor, Maine, when they were two and half years old. They swear they remember helping "push" Diver Ed into the water in his scuba suit. This event actually happened, and there are no pictures or video to help them re-create the memory all these years later. It was simply one of the most awesome experiences of their lives up to that point, so it stuck.

Hearing my boys tell stories about their earliest memories encourages me to help them remember even more about our amazing adventures. I want them to relive their wonder when they walked into the Hoh Rain Forest in Olympic National Park or scrambled up a rocky peak in Badlands National Park. Even though I know many experiences will fade away as they grow up, I want the seminal moments to stick. I want them to hold on to as much of the magic as possible. Here are some of the ways we've managed to capture our incredible camping memories over the years.

Before You Go

I taught third grade for ten years, so I can't help but bring some of that educational background into my parenting and travel planning. My kids will just have to deal with that for the rest of their lives. As teachers, we learn how important it is to create background knowledge before diving into any new novel or nonfiction book. The idea is that your students will get so much more out of *Henry's Freedom Box* if they already have a bit of knowledge about the Underground Railroad.

Fun Book Collections for Your Little Road-Trippers

- Good Night Our World series
- Where Is? series
- Who Was? series
- If You Lived at the Time series
- Ranger in Time series

From early on, I applied this concept to our family camping trips, and I'm convinced it's made a world of difference in how much my boys soak up when we visit a new place. When they were just toddlers, it was as simple as reading them *Good Night Maine* before heading up to Acadia National Park. As they got older, we would check out a stack of books from the library before heading off to historic Charleston, South Carolina, or Gettysburg National Military Park. Beyond the books, our boys love watching YouTube videos of a destination before we arrive. And we also try to find some audiobooks that touch on regional history or culture to fill our road-tripping hours. One of our favorite memories was listening to

I Survived the Eruption of Mount St. Helens, 1980 as we drove toward the national volcanic monument in Washington State.

I've found that it's important to keep the learning light and to keep it fun. We work hard to get them interested without being too teacherly about it. And we've seen this pay off big-time on our trips. The boys are always super excited to see the things we have been yammering on about for a few weeks. Plus, we get a head start on making those memories really stick by building some of that background knowledge in advance.

- - - - Famous Children's Book Characters Who Go Camping - - - -

- *Amelia Bedelia Goes Camping*
- *Curious George Goes Camping*
- *Maisy Goes Camping*
- *Just Me and My Dad* (Little Critter)
- *Flat Stanley Goes Camping*
- *Olivia Goes Camping*

Pictures, Pictures Everywhere

Of course, pictures are the way we all instinctively capture every single moment of our lives these days. With access to smartphones and digital cameras, we come back from camping trips with more pictures than we know how to manage.

The greatest irony is that many of these pictures just get buried in our camera rolls, never to be seen again. We are taking more pictures than ever before, but many of us never print out or display our greatest travel memories.

As hard as it is to find the time, we try to make the effort to get photos printed out in some manner. We've seen how framed images and photo books encourage our kids to relive our travel and camping highlights and truly secure those lifelong memories. Following are some of our favorite ways to get photos off our phones and into our everyday lives.

Old-School Photo Wallets

Remember those plastic photo wallets that our grandmothers used to carry around in their purses? It might surprise you to know that you can still buy them in drugstores or online. It might surprise you even more to know that this is one of our boys' favorite ways to organize photos from a family camping trip.

Years ago, we returned from a spring break camping trip to Charleston, South Carolina. Our older two children had an amazing time, and they wanted to bring in pictures to show their class at school. It was a Sunday night, and they desperately wanted to bring in the pictures the next day. Our local pharmacy has a one-hour photo department, so I let them each pick their twenty favorite images from the trip and went to pick them up. While at the store, I grabbed a few of those photo wallets and personalized the covers with their names, the trip, and the date.

This was one of their favorite mementos ever, and they frequently ask for more when we return from our camping trips. They get to pick the pictures, and it's their own album to keep in their bedroom or bring to school. I love when I catch one of the boys quietly flipping through an album from years ago.

Photo-Book Apps

Years ago, I saw some hilarious social media ads for the Chatbooks app that were effective enough to convince me to try the product. I'm so glad I did. I was impressed with my very first Chatbook and have continued to make them for all of our epic camping adventures. There are many popular photo-book apps, including Snapfish, Shutterfly, Mixbook, and Picaboo. I'll often use Shutterfly if I get a great coupon and I'm looking to create a nice, hardbound photo book. But I like the size and look of the Chatbooks, and I feel that they are particularly kid friendly. My boys love showing their friends the Chatbooks I've made for our Sleeping Bear Dunes trip or our latest vacation at Fort Wilderness Campground in Disney World.

I've gotten in the habit of creating a Chatbook while we're driving home from a family camping vacation. I can toggle easily between our multiple Instagram accounts, which is one of my favorite features. Having all our Chatbooks on a shelf in the family room at home, where our kids can flip through them on a regular basis, helps turn our camping trips into lifelong memories.

Scrapbooking

I was never a scrapbooker, and it's hard enough for me to get a photo book done, so I will probably never fully embrace this hobby. But I have seen so many family camping scrapbooks and, yes, I'm pretty jealous. The secret to success seems to be actually keeping the scrapbook in the camper and working on it throughout the trip. I have a friend who does this with her kids as a wind-down activity before bed every night. She has a small tackle box full of supplies, and she saves all their ticket stubs, hiking maps, leaves, or flowers from the day. What about the pictures, you might ask? She uses a portable photo printer to get the best pictures off her phone and into the scrapbook.

Another fun option is using the new generation of Polaroid-style cameras that have come back into fashion. We have a Fujifilm Instax Mini 9 that our boys love to use when we travel, so this is serious #CampingGoals for us.

Keeping Track of Your Adventures

When you love something so much, and you do it so often, experiences have a way of blending into each other. We have a few different methods of documenting our individual camping trips to help us remember things that might otherwise fade away.

Magnetic and Scratch-Off Maps

A ubiquitous item in the RV community is a map attached to the outside of the camper that displays which states you have visited. Some of these are peel-and-stick vinyl with magnetic states and others are permanent stickers. Different campers have their own rules for filling in a state on the map. Some folks only "claim" a state if they have actually camped there. Others will count a simple drive-through visit. Our personal sticker map includes all the states we have traveled to as a family, whether or not we brought the RV.

-------------------- **Five Favorite Travel Maps** --------------------

1. RV State Sticker Travel Map by Evolve Skins

2. US Travel Tracker Map by Rachel Alvarez Art

3. Magnetic Collectors Map and 50 State Collectible Magnets Box Set from Wall Drug Store (magnets sold separately)

4. Scratch Off USA Map Poster by Earthabitats

5. National Parks Explorers Map by Seth and Maddy Lucas

You don't have to own an RV to embrace the map tradition. You can find a variety of scratch-off maps that look great hanging in the house. We have a black-and-gold scratch-off map that features major landmarks across the country like the Statue of Liberty and Mount Rushmore. The boys love coming home from a camping trip and scratching off a new landmark. I also have my eyes on a fun national park map that includes stickers for each of the sixty-one national parks in America. There are even scratch-off maps for niche interests like visiting all the major-league baseball parks in the United States.

Passport to Your National Parks

On one of our earliest camping adventures to Acadia National Park, we bought a Passport to Your National Parks, a pocket-size booklet that has regional maps, park information, and space to record your park visits with stamps. Nearly every one of the NPS's 400-plus park units has a "cancellation station" where you find a unique park stamp and a date stamp.

Our boys love to run to the cancellation station and add a new stamp to our family passport book. They also enjoy flipping back through the passport and looking at all the stamps that we have collected over the years. Each stamp brings back memories and encourages storytelling, like remembering the scary Ape Caves of Mount St. Helens or the crystal-blue waters of Crater Lake.

Junior Ranger Vests, Hats, or Backpacks

If your kids are going to participate in the NPS Junior Ranger program, it's a good idea to keep track of all those badges and patches in some way. We didn't have a game plan for this early on, and those little suckers ended up spread out in random places throughout the RV, car, and house. It took us a while to realize that most people keep the collection together on one special article of clothing or accessory.

If you want to be official, there's an actual Junior Ranger vest that you can buy from the park service. But you don't have to purchase anything special. Some people use a hiking backpack or a jacket. We like the idea of a fishing hat the best. We bought large hats that the kids could grow into over the years, and they easily hang on hooks in the RV or at home.

Postcard Binder Rings

You know all those cool postcards you spot on your road trips? If you're like us, you buy a bunch and then never do anything with them. So we started a fun tradition years ago on our trip to the Pacific Northwest. Our boys were asking to buy postcards in gift shops. We told them that we would buy some if they wrote a note to themselves about a fun memory from the day and mailed it home. They enjoyed this activity and really loved coming home to their postcard collection from the trip. I punched a hole in the corner of each post-card and placed them on a binder ring. They both have a separate binder ring with postcards from each trip that they can flip through for years to come.

Campground Journal or Logbook ⊀ highly reccommend!

A lot of campers keep a camping journal or logbook in their car or RV and fill it out religiously on every trip. These journals not only preserve fun family memories, but they also prove to be really helpful when you are trying to remember the name of that campground you stayed at in Vermont five years ago. It's amazing how the details of even some of the best camping trips can start to fade over time.

You can purchase printed camping journals and logbooks online and in bookstores. There are also plenty of free templates that you can print out and copy for yourself. We happen to prefer using simple, blank Moleskine notebooks where we can record anything from site details to funny events or quotes from the trip.

··········· **What to Record in Your Camping Log** ···········

- ✧ campground name
- ✧ campground location
- ✧ site number and description
- ✧ favorite things about the campground
- ✧ least favorite things about

- the campground
- ✧ area attractions
- ✧ what you want to do on your next visit

Creating Meaningful Collections

The amount of stuff in my house is a regular source of stress for me. I happen to be a minimalist who wound up living with four maximalists. I truly understand their desire to bring home souvenirs and mementos from our camping trips. However, I also feel like many of these things just get lost in the shuffle and end up collecting dust bunnies in closets.

I like the popular saying about aiming to collect memories not things. The tricky part is that sometimes things really do help us remember special moments in our lives. I've tried to manage my family's love of collecting by focusing on looking for very specific mementos when we travel. We've found that certain types of souvenirs help us remember our trip without taking up too much space.

Magnets

Magnets have become our souvenir of choice for a variety of reasons. First of all, they don't take up a lot of space. They are also easy to find on our travels. Plus, they are perfect to display either in the camper or at home, providing great conversation starters about our trips. I love it when I catch my boys telling their friends about a particular magnet on our refrigerator. I'll never forget the time I heard one of their buddies say, "Wow! You've been to all these places?"

National Park Posters

There are a few print and poster series with similar styling that you can find in national parks across the country. We personally love the vintage WPA-style posters that have been popular in recent years. We don't find a great one at every single park we visit, but when we do, it's an exciting event. We have framed prints throughout our home from Acadia National Park, Great Smoky Mountains, Sleeping Bear Dunes, and many other favorite family destinations. We remember the most amazing adventures we have had every time we walk into these rooms.

Puzzles

Puzzles are another type of gift-shop souvenir that earn the space they take up in the game closet. Many of our favorite destinations have puzzle options for every age group, and we have found that our kids will return to them again and again. Putting together a puzzle of Mount Rushmore encourages them to relive the memories of that awesome family camping adventure.

Great Travel Print Collections

- ✧ See America by Creative Action Network
- ✧ Fifty-Nine Parks Collection
- ✧ Illustrated American Travel Collection by Anderson Design Group
- ✧ National Park Posters by Rob Decker
- ✧ Parks Project

⛶

The time we spend with our kids matters, whether they remember every single detail or not. Even though Jeremy and I know that's true, it's still important to us create collective family memories, the ones we will be talking about decades from now. We've found that a bit of extra effort in the memory-making department pays off big-time. In fact, our boys sometimes seem to remember more than we do.

Capturing camping memories can be as simple as printing up a photo book from an app or as elaborate as crafting scrapbooks around the RV dinette in the evenings. Find whatever works for you, and start recording those stories that your kids will remember and retell for years to come.

Afterword

STEPHANIE & JEREMY

When we first became parents, it felt like the onslaught of clichés would never stop. People told us that "they grow up so fast," that we "really had our hands full," and that it was all "just a stage." The very worst was when someone would tell us to "enjoy every minute." Guess what? When your babies keep you up *all night long*, you have our permission to not enjoy those minutes. Just surviving them will earn you a big high five from our little corner of the world.

As the years have passed, however, one cliché has revealed itself to hold the very kernel of parenting truth: the days are long, but the years are short.

There have been so many times when it seemed like we were crawling to the finish line at the end of the day, and yet a decade of parenting went by in a flash. We are closer to the year our twins will go off to college than we are to the year they were born. It's the truth, but it's barely comprehensible to us.

The days creep by, containing all the sibling fights, stomach viruses, and endless heaps of laundry. The years, though, they fly by, jam-packed with hiking adventures in Acadia National Park, epic road trips to South Dakota, and spring breaks in Texas Hill Country.

Our camping life has turned the blur of passing time into a virtual scrapbook of unforgettable family moments. These memories have been created in cabins, tents, and RVs all over this beautiful continent. The landscape changes. Vehicles and RVs get swapped and traded. But we are always there in those pictures, parents with three rapidly growing kids and our sweet rescued camping dog. There we all are, together at some campground, somewhere in the country.

⌗

Are we a happy family? Depends on the moment in which you ask. We want the best possible life for our boys, but sometimes we lose the thread. We fight. Our kids fight. We struggle with all of the big and small issues that families are dealing with everywhere. Plus, our boys leave their towels on the bathroom floor every dang day.

The days can be a challenge. But the years? The years are happier than we ever imagined they could be. We took a chance on writing a family story that included hundreds of magical nights spent around the campfire. And we are forever grateful that our bet paid off.

Our hope is that we have hundreds more days together with our kids at the campground.

Maybe we'll see you there.

Acknowledgments

To the entire RV Atlas community, we thank you so much for tuning into our weekly podcasts, reading our articles, and hanging out with us online and at the campground. Some of you have been following along with us on this journey for almost a decade, and your support and encouragement has meant everything. Your emails, notes, and comments keep us excited about creating new camping content week in and week out.

A special thanks to Kerri Cox, Kate Dunbar, and Casita Dean May for your incredible contributions to our podcasts and online community. Your nonstop encouragement and amazing content means the world to us.

Thanks to Emily Burton, who reached out at just the right time, with just the right skills and patiently helped us through some of our worst growing pains.

And thanks to David Blackmon, mostly for showing up at a Texas campground with bags of tacos and inspirational advice, but also for stepping in and taking over the thankless job of website design and tech support.

Thank you to the RV, camping, and outdoor industry partners who have supported the creation of the content in this book. We hoped to build a brand that spoke to a new generation of campers, and you believed in our voice.

The marketing team and product managers at Jayco have been an endless source of education, inspiration, and partnership. We have been so blessed to work particularly with Ashley Lehman, Renee Jones, Leah Jean Rassi, John Fisher, Matt Fisher, Chris Barth, Mike Aplin, Brent Hamood, and Amy Duthie. Working with Amanda Popp and the rest of the Bass Pro Shops and Cabela's team has been an amazing opportunity for us. There are some folks who just get what The RV Atlas is all about, and Amanda is one of those very special people.

Thanks to the whole Go RVing crew that we've worked with over the years, but especially to Courtney Bias, Karen Redfern, and Kevin Broom. You all are so, so smart. But you're also super funny, and most of the time that matters more. Thanks to Andy Bialorucki and Kelly Robertson, who we will someday take to lunch at Zimmermans, hand to heart.

We have to give a special thanks to the universe for finding us the most fabulous agent in all of the world, who then tracked down the most fabulous editor in all of the world. Marilyn Allen was patient beyond measure as we juggled parenting and work and tried to squeeze in time to write a book proposal. When we were ready, she was waiting. And Anna Michels, who is our dream editor because she is our perfect reader. We know it's just a matter of time before we see them both at the campground.

Index

W

Y

About the Authors

STEPHANIE PUGLISI is the cocreator of The RV Atlas Podcast Network, a boutique media company that creates content for camping and RV enthusiasts. She is also the coauthor of *Idiot's Guides: RV Vacations*. Stephanie produces the weekly podcast *The RV Atlas* and is a regular contributor to *Trailer Life* magazine. She imagines that her happy place would be reading in a hammock at the campground, but she's been too busy running after her three sons to try it out.

JEREMY PUGLISI is an English and film teacher and past winner of his school's Teacher of the Year award. He is also cohost of *The RV Atlas* podcast and coauthor of *Idiot's Guides: RV Vacations*. He has appeared on television more than fifty times as a spokesman for the RV industry and for Bass Pro Shops and Cabela's, where he proudly serves as a Pro Staff member. He loves nothing more than camping with Stephanie and his three sons, and he is always ready to hitch up and head out for the next adventure.

You can follow Jeremy and Stephanie's camping adventures @jeremy_and_stephanie on Instagram and @TheRVAtlas everywhere else.